SOFTWARE DEVELOPER LIFE

SOFTWARE DEVELOPER LIFE

DAVID XIANG

Software Developer Life

ISBN paperback: 978-1-7323459-0-4

ISBN ebook: 978-1-7323459-1-1

FIRST EDITION

To my father who has given me underrated career
advice over the years and to my mother who
got me through my first C class.

Contents

Acknowledgments

Thank you to all my friends who have shared their stories.

0: Introduction

We've made a dent into the 21st century and software has been eating the world. Suspenseful tech dramas play out in the news, boot camps churn out entry-level developers in a matter of months, and there's even an HBO show dedicated to Silicon Valley. In the midst of these trends lies a severe lack of attention to the daily life of the developer—the day-to-day reality that surrounds each line of code. There are plenty of resources available to help the budding developer learn how to code, but what about everything else?

My name is Dave Xiang. I grew up in suburban Massachusetts. My extra time went into playing Starcraft and leveling up Everquest characters. My extra money went into playing Dance Dance Revolution at the local arcade. I majored in Electrical/Computer Engineering (ECE) at Carnegie Mellon (CMU), got a job straight out of college as a firmware developer, and transitioned into full software-mode a few years later. Though I am no veteran developer, I've been through the paces in my eight years as a professional and have held a number of distinct developer roles.

Let me give you some backstory. This all began with a video I uploaded to YouTube way back in 2013. Like every Millennial, I wanted to *do something*. It started off with an embarrassing vlog, a couple breakdancing demo reels, and then I uploaded a video explaining the basics of RAM. I didn't think much of it at the time, but it was well received. The video didn't go viral exactly, but it gave me an idea, a hint of *potential*.

A few years and a bunch of uploads later, and I've built a decent fan base of ~40K subscribers. My content reflects all that I've learned throughout my career, packing significant personal experiences into short, vlog-style videos. My aim was to create a space where people could come learn about new technologies and get a better understanding of life as a professional programmer. The many positive comments online I've received have kept me motivated.

I am not an illustrious coder—I haven't created my own programming language, and I don't have a white wizard's beard. I've held a handful of cookie-cutter software jobs and have a knack for story-telling. As such, this book aims to help students, new professionals, and anyone looking for a sneak peek inside the world of software.

With respect to my content, the analytics never lie. My softer content consistently gets more watch time than my technical videos. The stuff about daily life, interview rejections, and "How to be a Better Programmer" have always resonated more with viewers.

Throughout this book I have drawn on personal experiences, but it is also filled with many perspectives and unique stories from my friends. I went around and interviewed everyone I know that is, or has ever worked with, a software developer. Everyone has a special story to tell and a wealth of advice to share. Their names may have been changed but their stories never will.

This book consists of 40 chapters. Each chapter is influenced by someone's experience in the tech world. I've included a mix of concrete advice, abstract meta-principles, and entertaining stories. Each chapter belongs to one of five categories:

1. Career
2. Learning
3. Coding
4. Daily Life
5. Stories

This book is a highlight reel of software development life. Enjoy!

—David Xiang

1: Peer-Vs.-Peer [Stories]

Every fall, Carnegie Mellon University hosts a job fair called the Technical Opportunities Conference (TOC). For many students, this event is a counter-productive stretch of two hours that leaves people feeling unexpectedly depressed about their future. The university's student center fills up with job booths while hordes of students wait in line to speak with a handful of company reps. The reps are usually CMU alumni looking to fill their hiring pipeline with fellow Tartans.

The competition is stiff and more often than not, the conference provides students with zero productive leads. Regardless, CMU recommends that everyone attend. We practice wearing our over-sized suits, get an opportunity to professionally present ourselves, and get a taste of the fabled real world that's waiting for us outside university grounds. This conference purposefully promotes peer competition and serves as an unbiased progress marker for students; how well you navigate the booths reflects your current aptitude.

Looking back, it's impressive the difference one year makes for the typical undergraduate.

Looking back, it's impressive the difference one year makes for the typical undergraduate. As a freshman, the non-introductory classes the sophomores are taking seem light years away. Sophomores get jealous of the shiny internships that the juniors are getting. Once you're a junior, seniors taking their capstone projects and getting fat job offers start to intimidate you. By the time you're a senior, you grudgingly bow your head to seasoned professionals with real jobs, even though some of them are no more than a year or two older than you.

NVIDIA always had a cutthroat presence at the TOC. Founded in 1993, NVIDIA is a living legend in Silicon Valley and they are still killing it today. At CMU, they gained TOC-notoriety through the use of a simple but terrifying 3-question quiz.

There were two flavors of quiz, Analog and Digital, each capable of demoralizing the unsuspecting underclassmen. These quizzes were NVIDIA's way of rooting out the incompetent: an easy and effective way to filter down the magnitude of students pouring through their booth. When I took them, the analog quiz covered voltage differentials and asked you to explain what an amplifier was doing. The digital quiz made you map out some gates, reason through some logic, and enumerate a truth table.

You never really fail the quiz, you just fail yourself. Once you get to the front of the queue, you're handed your questions and ushered into a staging area of standing desks. Around you, any number of sweaty students are staring pale-faced at their own test sheets. After filling out the questionnaire, you wait in line again to review your responses with an official NVIDIA judge. Overlay this whole scene with a subtle but very clear power differential between student and employer, and you should have a good picture painted in your head of what this tech-based cattle market is like.

First time around, I failed myself. I looked at the quiz, realized I couldn't do any of the problems, and quietly excused myself from the booth. I was doing everyone a favor—one less person in line for the other students and one less incompetent prospector to discourage for NVIDIA. I'll *always* remember that moment; as I walked away, I felt the laser burn of all those eyes following me out of the booth.

Fast-forward one year. I was a budding junior; a little smarter but still hating the TOC. First things first, I headed straight back to NVIDIA, because I remembered the questions and *thought* I knew the answers. This time, I finished the quiz and made it to the final line. Unfortunately, it turned out I still didn't know the answers; I scored about a 1.5/3 and proceeded to botch my interview with the NVIDIA rep. My résumé went straight into the please-do-not-call-back-these-students pile. I would have been crushed except that I saw underclassmen doing the *exact* same thing I did the year before. They picked up the quiz, looked very sad, and quietly left the booth. I wanted to give them all hugs.

After some more running around futilely handing out résumés, I bumped into an ex-girlfriend from my sophomore year. She was with her new boyfriend, Mike. By the way, CMU is filled with Asian-American Mikes who

play basketball, dominate at Street Fighter, and are incredibly smart. He was the same major as me, one year
younger, and had already worked at Microsoft. *Damn,
she upgraded!* Let me remind you again of the CMU student dynamic and mindset. Big company internships are
coveted; the people who land them are the cream of the
crop. Fancy internships are on people's minds 24/7, so
naturally I was jealous of Mike. When we bumped into
each other, my ex-girlfriend graciously asked:

> "Hey Mike, do you think you could help get Dave
> an interview at   Microsoft?"

> "Maybe. Is he smart?"

The exchange was lightning quick and I got an influx of different emotions. It was a mix of shock, sadness, and *damn this guy.* Mike looked at my résumé, came to the conclusion that I hadn't taken the right classes yet, and decided he couldn't help me. *Did I just get pseudo-rejected by Mike?*

I don't have a name for this feeling, but I'll describe it for you. Something happens to you that doesn't seem like a big deal at first. The day goes by and you dwell on it more and more with each passing hour. Before long, your day is ruined. Let's call it the "increasingly unfortunate hindsight emotional trauma due to crappy person and interaction feeling."

> *I would stop putting the better engineers on a pedestal and begin to wean my mind off inter-student comparisons.*

A day later, I finally stopped thinking about Mike and made an important decision. I would stop putting the better engineers on a pedestal and begin to wean my mind off inter-student comparisons. It wasn't easy to do; peer competition is rampant in any engineering school in the U.S. We compete with our classmates for the most elegant coding solutions, the top test scores, and the best internships. One of my CMU courses would publicly post everyone's coding scores on the class website. Everyone used aliases, but we all knew who was at the top. The TAs made sure you knew who wrote better code than you. This was the kind of competition we had to deal with on a daily basis.

Whether they admit it or not, CMU breeds a cut-throat environment. On the one hand, the peer-vs.-peer competition pushes everyone hard; if you respond well to this kind of atmosphere, you quickly rise to the top of your game. On the other hand, it's a little messed up.

My biggest takeaway from this experience is that you can't let another person's progression disturb you from yours. There will always be students like Mike; they're younger than you, ahead of you in class, and smarter than you. Extrapolate this idea out beyond academics. Each one of us is on our own timeline. Taking random samplings of timelines out of context is never helpful. Your 25-year-old self is probably not comparable to 25-year-old Bill Gates. Don't dwell on this, but use it for discretionary doses of motivation. As long as you—and only you—continue to progress, everything is on the right track.

2: Technical Foundation [Learning]

Understanding the basics is the key to software development. I will go further and claim that it is the key to every single profession. The significance of fundamentals is frequently underestimated and often neglected. People tend to associate this with being easy, but there is nothing easy about it. I like to encompass these values and their importance with one word—foundation.

A solid foundation can support the tallest buildings. Foundational ideas form the basis for complex theories and they enable the extensions of novel ideas. For any field, the people at the highest level are the ones who deeply understand foundation; that's why they can break it sometimes. To this day, I am still self-conscious about my fundamentals. Getting a refresher from an old textbook is never something to be embarrassed about.

At CMU, I spent 150 dollars to purchase a Computer Systems textbook that I barely read as I scrambled to keep up with lectures. It wasn't until I started working that I began to fully appreciate its content. I've broken its bindings from too much page flipping and it has never failed to deliver me technical guidance in times of need.

The first—and perhaps most difficult—step is pinpointing areas where we've missed the basics. During my first couple years of college, I often found myself staring blankly at coding assignments. Things didn't make sense. I had missed a fundamental concept.

During academic life, curriculums and course progressions can assist with pinpointing weak areas in our foundation. If we fudge some code or bomb a test, we know something has gone over our heads. Retracing old homework and lecture notes is never a bad place to start. The most significant value an engineering school can offer its students lies in its curriculum—your learning has been organized for you. After entering post-academic life, shaping your progression gets harder. You don't have convenient, "Move on to Part 3.4" markers to guide you. In real life, all the knowledge is out there, it's just not served straight up for you on a platter.

For any field, the people at the highest level are the ones who deeply understand foundation; that's why they can break it sometimes.

I preach foundation often, and I'll preach it again, I'm sure. Always, always make sure you understand the fundamentals. If you're learning something for the first time, be completely honest with yourself about your level. If you think you've grown beyond the fundamental concepts, go back and re-read them; you will always uncover more nuances. At CMU, I tricked myself into *thinking* that I understood pointers. Reality kicked in when I got into the labs for linked lists and trees. I couldn't wrap my head around pointers to pointers. Is a pointer a memory address? Is it a variable? Is it both? What's this deep copying thing?

You will inevitably fall behind in your engineering classes. The reason for this is that these courses focus on content over pacing. An engineering course's definition of pacing is simple—students do whatever it takes to keep up. Each course is packed with content, and rightfully so. This may sound discouraging, but everyone is in the same boat. Professors have only a limited amount of time to teach you; it's up to you to sufficiently allocate and utilize your time to ensure you understand the material. And if you don't, then seek help from the faculty. That's what they're there for! Remember, you'll never have the opportunity to pick the brains of these people again once you leave. Good teachers want you to learn as much as they know.

Understanding the basics is essential. Just like a tall building, our technical foundation needs upkeep and must be periodically reinforced. Here are a few tips and tricks that may help.

Basic Idea

We must have a complete understanding of even the simplest things. Fundamental principles, ideas, and methods have to be mastered. This results in a solid knowledge foundation, which is everything.

Revisit Often

Once is never enough. There is *always* a concept that you can understand better by examining it again.

Blank Document Test

Open up a blank document on your computer. Do not refer to anything and write an outline of any concept you're trying to understand. If you can't write anything, then you don't understand it at all.

Focus on Sub-Problems

Do not tackle huge issues in their entirety. Find a sub-problem and understand it completely. Each complicated subject has a handful of core ideas. Isolate each one and figure out how it contributes to the whole.

When You're Stuck

If you find yourself stuck on a particular concept, ask yourself: is there a simpler concept beneath this that you do not fully understand? For example, if you're struggling to understand how buffer overflow works, is it because you haven't grasped function call stacks? Train yourself to pinpoint that more fundamental concept quickly. Once you're proficient at digging down to the simpler concept beneath, you will rarely get stuck and your progression will accelerate.

> *If you find yourself stuck on a particular concept, ask yourself: is there a simpler concept beneath this that you do not fully understand?*

How Does A Computer Work?

I often meet developers who can write code but don't understand the basics of a computer. It's easy to get your program up and running and have the system do its thing, but it makes a huge difference if you understand what the computer is doing with your software. How does the operating system switch over to your code? What kind of resources is your software utilizing? Software is the highest interface we have to computers. There is a colossal stack underneath it which controls how electrons flow through metal and travel around the world. The more you understand that, the more empowered you will be as a developer.

Conclusion

Throughout your progression, stay true to your level. Not only is this a good practice in humility, but it is also good training for your brain. When you're at a low level, you should be eager to ingest more knowledge and level up. When you're at a high level, you should be eager to accept re-affirmations to reinforce your foundation. Learning is meta—there is a lot to learn about learning itself. Stay humble and open-minded and the world is your oyster!

3: Writing Emails [Daily Life]

Every position has a set of ideal traits. The relentless salesperson makes 9,000 calls a day, stays positive through endless rejections, and burns the midnight oil prospecting. The pixel-perfect designer mocks out every edge case, stays aligned with the vision, and keeps up patient dialogues with impatient customers. And what about the developer? We think clearly, communicate effectively, and build mission-critical applications. Sound a little too good to be true? Well I did say they were *ideal*.

Let's dissect one of these attributes—clarity of mind. Every trait we possess is ultimately measured by the external perception of others; your self-perception and self-confidence can only validate your skills up to a point. To put it simply—what your colleagues think of you matters, a *lot*. This is our personal brand.

Wait a second. Doesn't this idea of personal branding go at odds with the age-old lesson of not worrying about what other people think of you? Be careful. Not worrying about what others think of you does not give you a free pass to do as you wish and behave haphazardly. In our professional and personal lives, we must put our best foot forward, and then let the people around us settle in with their own conclusions. You'll never be able to control the judgements of others so don't get attached to it. Keep things simple and you will surprise yourself with its positive results. Put in work, add value,

> *Not worrying about what others think of you does not give you a free pass to do as you wish and behave haphazardly.*

and there won't be anything to worry about.

Our personal brand is rooted in two things: raw value and how we express ourselves. Your value as a developer is easily measured. Code well, execute consistently, and be a team player. We'll talk more about coding later, but for now, let's focus on personal brand. Your brand is developed through how you express yourself. One of the most overlooked forms of expression is how you write emails. Emails are pervasive and directly showcase one's clarity of mind. Just like your code, everything you write must be done effectively, thoughtfully, and with intention.

Context

The context—or Slide 0—must be presented first. Don't make any assumptions about your recipient's understanding of what's going on. Paint the picture for your audience and do it in less than three sentences.

Formatting

The power of visual formatting must not be underestimated. There's a reason why we're picky about diff tools, enjoy JSON parsers, and code up pretty() functions. With emails, formatting is essential and must be used purposefully; basic gram-mar, spell-checking, new-lines, and text-modifiers are necessities.

There are a few tech-niques that are worth men-tioning. <u>Underlining</u> is useful

There are no hard rules. Your style of writing, coding, and thinking will always be your own.

for creating contextual titles, breaking up long text, and providing helpful highlights. **Bold** is an amazing mod-ifier that can direct attention, emphasize points, and create clear call-to-actions. Finally, let's not forget about the versatile and ubiquitous list. Lists are universally un-derstood, flexible, easy on the eyes, and automatically organize your thoughts. What are the potential solutions for this new authentication feature? Well, here are three options: A, B, and C. Lists also give your recipients a convenient way to respond quickly to your suggestions:

"Joe, I think option C is alright, B is subpar, and A is money!"

There are no hard rules. Your style of writing, coding, and thinking will always be your own. As you develop and write your thoughts down, stay conscious of formatting; it's one of many tools on your belt for effective written communication. Develop your style, be consistent with it, and make your work an easy read for everyone.

Expectation

All your emails must have a clear expectation. If you need a specific response, ask politely and directly. If it's an FYI email, clearly put [Memo] in the message so there isn't any awkward obligation for a response. What are *you* looking to get out of this email? Just checking up on a deadline? Disseminating critical information? Simple status update? Looking for feedback? An expectation must be set.

Stay Warm

"Hope you've been having a great week" goes a long way.

Appropriate Usage

Email is one of many mediums of communication and has its own time and place. When do we not use emails? If you need a simple response, send a direct message, or take a walk across the office. If you expect heavy discussion, organize a meeting instead of starting a snowballing thread. If you need something ASAP, make a phone call, leave a message, and contemplate why anything would need to be so urgent. Appropriate discretion and tact should surround every form of communication.

Add Value to a Thread

If you work at a large company, you'll witness the phenomenon of the snowballing email chain. These are giant threads where employees play hot potato and respond with convenient one-liners that add zero value:

+Bob. Bob knows about this module. Cheers,

—George

Cheers for nothing, George. Do *not* do this. If there's an expectation for you to respond, then do so with value. If you have to pass the potato, pass it with class. Do the homework and explain why Bob is better suited to answer the question. Furthermore, give Bob the context and information he needs to respond. Bob will appreciate the gesture and won't have to scrub through the massive chain. Eighty-five percent of people on these threads add nothing to the discussion; do not be one of those people.

Real-Life Alignment

Keep the tone of your emails aligned with your real-life behavior. Your word is your word, and your offline and online personas must be consistent. Acting boisterously in emails only to become passive aggressive in real life is a bad look. People's digital perception of you must make sense when they speak with you directly. If you really feel the need to anonymously troll, Reddit will always be there for you.

Conclusion

Emails are a low-pressure, asynchronous way to communicate. Use them to generate thoughtful responses that do not require immediate action. Emails allow people to read, digest, and respond in their own time. Compose emails well, use them appropriately, and remember to give your Slide 0 context. Everyone will nod their heads at your well-organized thoughts and you will earn the respect of your colleagues.

4: The Angry Guy [Coding]

One person's beloved design pattern is another person's hated anti-pattern. For everything that you believe is awesome, there is a person out there who thinks it's garbage. Opinions aside, the number one complaint among my friends in software has always been the same—the aggressive, angry, big-headed developer. There's always one wherever you work, and the character attributes are almost always the same. This is someone who has a wealth of knowledge and possesses awesome technical chops, but

> *For everything that you believe is awesome, there is a person out there who thinks it's garbage.*

stays stubbornly bullish about *their* way being the best. At best, they become an inconvenience to work with, and at worst a genuine reason to quit the job.

As developers, we must strive to write exceptional code, keep an open mind towards others, and not become the aggressive developer. Software development is hard, but most of the time the hard part isn't the coding—it's working with other developers. Dealing with big egos and rigid personalities can be stressful for everyone. Luckily, there are strategies to handle such challenges.

Fighting Fire with Fire Never Works

An ancient Taoist teaching says it best—you never fight fire with fire. It's a very simple lesson that is easy to follow as long as you control your emotions. If a boisterous developer enjoys yelling, you'll achieve nothing yelling back. One of these personalities is difficult enough; having two of them can be disastrous. There are other ways to deal with this.

Let Them Talk with The Right Questions

An aggressive developer will be bullish with his or her opinions. It might be a naming convention, specific third-party libraries, a language, or tabs versus spaces. Stubbornness tends to follow the aggression. These developers aren't ones to easily back down from their opinions, even if you've spotted legitimate cracks. When you're on the receiving end of this, clarifying questions work well to gain insights into the other person's thoughts and can potentially disarm their position peacefully.

It's smoother for them to re-rationalize their argument rather than accept an unwelcome critique from you.

A great question to ask is, "Could you help me understand this part better?" Two things happen in this question. First, you showcase humility by qualifying the question with your mental slowness. It's not the aggressive

22

developer's opinion, it's just you not being able to keep up. Second, no one minds explaining their own thoughts further to help someone else understand them better. If someone takes offense to this question, you have met a true jerk.

Another similar question to ask is, "Could you clarify this part?" This is slightly more direct than our previous example, but its purpose is the same. The goal here is for you to selectively direct the developer's attention to the cracks. It's smoother for them to re-rationalize their argument rather than accept an unwelcome critique from you. You might not have to do any arguing at all.

During Disagreements

Inevitably, any software development team will have some conflict. When this happens, your approach is very important; you must never disparage the opinions of others. If you talk another's opinion down, you've bought yourself a one-way ticket to a grudge. A dispute over a software design pattern should never turn into resentment between colleagues.

During a technical disagreement, there will be a con for every pro you're fighting for, and the same goes for your counterparty. You can't target the bad parts of someone else's opinions, only to stay conveniently unaware of the bad parts of your own. Your opinion has its own flaws and a technical decision will never be black-or-white, it's merely the best choice you can make to solve a particular problem given a particular circumstance. Disagreements are productive conversations in disguise—use a peaceful approach to uncover them.

Do Not Silo Them

Do not isolate the aggressive developer! I made this mistake when I was managing a hot-headed programmer at my last job. It was the easy—but incorrect—way of handling the situation.

One of our star developers was getting out of hand, forcefully pushing his design principles onto his fellow developers. The team had become frustrated and our collaboration was slowly deteriorating. Instead of solving the issue as a team, I decided to silo the aggressive developer. My thinking was that I would minimize his interaction with the team, keep him producing code, and enable a safer atmosphere for the other developers.

Unfortunately, the developer took this as a green light to start doing everything his way. He no longer felt any obligation to sync up and used this new independence as a trump card for technical decisions. He proceeded to re-write people's code out from under them and wreaked havoc across development.

The team was now even more frustrated. Someone they had zero contact with was hindering their development. Before, they could at least interact with him! Eventually, we had to let that developer go, even though he was one of the strongest technologists at our company. As the manager at the time, I take full responsibility for that unfortunate outcome. It was a great learning experience for me, and I hope this mini-story can show you what *not* to do if you're ever in this situation.

Keep Your Mind Open & Watch Out for the Halo Effect

The big-headed developer that you can't stand might inadvertently be caught in a vicious psychological cycle by his or her peers—you. This can be caused by a phenomenon known as the Halo Effect. This is when your initial impression of someone influences every single thought you have about him or her thereafter. For example, someone rubs you the wrong way during their first month on the job, then all of a sudden *everything* they do starts to annoy you. You had one heated argument over table schema, and all of a sudden, this person seems grossly incompetent.

Always be aware of your bias and remember that no one is all good, or all bad.

If this sounds familiar, take a step back and keep your cognitive bias in check; that aggressive developer is not a bad person. Keep an open mind at work because it's extremely easy to develop a Halo Effect for everyone around you. Always be aware of your bias and remember that no one is all good, or all bad. You yourself might be seen as that huge incompetent fool at any time in any position throughout your career.

Dynamic Relationships

Every relationship has a different tone. This is a natural part of life; your dynamic with your sorority sisters isn't going to be the same as the one with your office colleagues. While it's normal to switch up your tone, your core personality must remain consistent.

A recurring theme with angry developers is the personality switch. They might be very warm towards you, but then quickly change personas and disparage another colleague. They are cordial in a meeting with the boss, but rudely criticize code behind closed doors. This looks bad in any professional setting. If this sounds like you, be careful.

Conclusion

You will encounter many unique personalities in your career; the angry and bullish developer will show up all over the place. Remember that it's unfair to typecast anyone as the bad developer—every situation you encounter will be different, with different people, under different circumstances. Even though the technology will always be your craft, you can't neglect the inter-personal aspects of working in software. Behind all the code, there are the people that wrote it, and behind every person, there is an ego.

5: Into The Deep [Stories]

This story was told to me by my friend Patrick, a mobile developer and fellow CMU brother-in-arms. Patrick is two years my senior and made the switch from mechanical engineering to software development shortly after graduating. Pat is known for throwing himself into new environments. His free-spirited nature applied to engineering classes as well as our social life; parties were always more fun when Pat was around. Patrick's unfettered approach to the unknown inspired me to push myself harder at CMU.

When you read about Pat's learning style, you may find that it goes at odds with my previous championing of basics, fundamentals, and foundation. If you find yourself paralyzed with next steps, a full-force jump is a great springboard into learning something new. However, this is only the entry point. It is not—by any means—a substitute for the basics; it is just a start.

The pressure is on, crashing and burning is a possibility, and leveling up is a certainty

The easiest way to learn is to jump into the deep end without knowing how to swim. This is the WordPress veteran signing a contract to write a Rails app for the first time. This is you stumbling into a new job that you are grossly unqualified for. The pressure is on, crashing and burning is a possibility, and leveling up is a certainty.

Back during CMU, I went through this repeatedly. I have vivid memories of every engineering class. If it wasn't the excruciating amount of work, it was the eccentric professor, the jerk teaching assistant (TA), or the progressively challenging exams—there was always something. However, these sensations of drowning would inevitably turn into a dawning realization that I'd gained tremendous amounts of knowledge. I call this forceful learning. It's an amazing way to grow as long as you can deal with the high levels of stress that come with it.

As a mechanical engineer, I decided to take a class in computer-aided design from the Computer Science (CS) Department. The class description had something about 3-D modeling in it. I signed up with the support of some rational logic: *3-D modeling kind of sounds like 3-D printers, and 3-D printers are related to mechanical engineering, right? Sounds reasonable—sure.* I had no idea what I was getting into, but I wasn't going to leave CMU without taking at least one CS course.

First day of class rolled around and the professor handed us the syllabus. It turned out that we'd be developing a full suite of 3-D modeling software from scratch. Immediately, I realized I was in way over my head. I hadn't given the course description more than a cursory glance; I wasn't expecting there to be *that* much coding involved. I was hoping for some nice hand-holding like the tutorials I found on the Internet. This class had barely any lectures. The semester was going to be dominated by coding labs. Luckily, I had been through these enough times in the past and my engineering mindset kicked in.

The first assignment was to render Mickey Mouse. We were given two things—a massive dump of XYZ coordinates and a deadline. There wasn't a friendly student forum to discuss homework. There weren't regular office hours. The homework assignment itself barely counted as an instructional document. All we had was a huge cloud of obscurity—something very normal for a CMU CS course. This was a short interaction I had with a TA:stor

"Hey, which language should we use?"

"Whatever you're comfortable with. Java or C++ should work."

"Ok. Is there anything we can download? A homework template or something?"

"Template?! No templates here. You should be able to compile your source and execute it."

"Ok. Are there any progress markers? How will I know if I'm on the right track?"

"You'll know you're on the right track when you render Mickey Mouse. We just need to visually *see* Mickey by Friday. Also, this is the easiest assignment."

Now, you might be thinking that doesn't sound so bad, nothing too strenuous for a coder, but let me give you an idea of where I was coming from. I was a mechanical engineer who at that time had yet to take a single programming course at CMU. How was I even let into this course? I'm not really sure to be honest—it's all a blur. I had done a tiny amount of programming back in high school, but nothing like what was expected of me here. How do you even get a C++ project started? What's GCC? What's a Make file? Should I use Java? What's the JVM? I don't have Linux installed, am I screwed?

*... it's sometimes the complete **lack** of training and resources that makes CMU, CMU*

You see what I mean? I was a total noob. Luckily for me, Google had been invented and I had a lot of stamina. After a sleepless week, I pulled through and delivered one rendered Mickey Mouse. I'd never been so happy to see a Disney character on a screen before. I remember the day I got that mouse to show up, I felt like there was a holy light shining down on my computer.

CMU is known for having one of the best engineering programs in the world. People think we have the best teachers, the most thorough training, and the most highly accessible resources. However, it's sometimes the complete *lack* of training and resources that makes CMU, CMU. Tenured professors come to campus twice a week, give a couple obscure lectures, then disappear before their TAs can hand out crazy homework assignments. Despite the "world-class" program, there isn't as much structure as you may think.

Jumping into the deep end is an amazing way to learn. There will be times in your life when you'll have the opportunity to put yourself through forceful learning or take the easy way out. I recommend everyone try the forceful way. Just remember to jump with discretion; that feeling of drowning can turn into real drowning if you're not careful.

This is academic pressure and growth. What happens when you don't work your ass off? You fail. How about a nice textbook and a list of resources? You're lucky we have Google. Implementation guidelines? Choose whatever programming language you like. Can't code? You can always drop out. We got used to two simple things—expect nothing and execute everything.

6: Fifteen Minutes Dictate A Year [Career]

Throughout life, we periodically find ourselves in the middle of crucial conversations. Whether they're personal or professional, they all have one thing in common—they have a direct impact on our lives. You will have many of these conversations throughout your life and you will undoubtedly mess many them up, but you will grow from them, and, more importantly, you will never forget them.

Keep in mind that importance will always be relative; you might be sweating over a performance review, but it's just another day-to-day meeting for your manager.

The crucial conversations I'm going focus on will be in the context of your career in software development. The conversations will fall along a spectrum. The big, stressful, scary conversations come during final interview rounds and nail-biting salary negotiations. The easy ones might land in your lap during an honest, open conversation with your boss.

A casual chat with the boss might blindside you, but most of the time, you'll have time to prepare. Always be mindful of when a crucial conversation is about to happen. Keep in mind that importance will always be relative; you might be sweating over a performance review, but it's just another day-to-day meeting for your manager.

You must be prepared for every crucial conversation, because they can affect your entire *life*. A fifteen-minute conversation about your salary will dictate what hits your bank account for an entire year. Preparedness is paramount and this chapter can help.

What Do You Want?

As a prerequisite, we must understand what we really want. Friends and family are useful resources, but at the end of the day, only you can define what you want. Always keep the concept of alignment in the back of your head. The big objectives in your life should align with your day-to-day conversations and activities. None of us have a straight path to our own personal North Star, but as long as we think about align-

> *If you lack the clarity of thought to divulge your own wants and needs, you will inevitably have an unproductive conversation with your counterparty.*

ment, we won't fall into the trap of drifting. According to Napoleon Hill—pioneering self-help author and author of "Think and Grow Rich"—drifting is the absolute worst thing you can do to yourself. Easy for me to say, but obviously, very difficult to do. We can struggle with this together.

Let's take the example of learning how to code. Learning how to code is just an activity, but what is your main objective? Break this down. Do you want to become a full-time software developer and make a career out of it? Do you want to level up your technical chops so you can be more literate with computers? Do you want to learn to code just to prototype your disruptive business idea? Your objective will dictate how you pursue your learning. It will influence who you reach out to, what you talk to them about, and the journey you have ahead of you.

How does this relate to crucial conversations? Understanding what you want is the first prerequisite to a successful crucial conversation. If you lack the clarity of thought to divulge your own wants and needs, you will inevitably have an unproductive conversation with your counterparty.

Let's pretend you're thinking about quitting your job. Your boss is aware of this and has scheduled a one-on-one with you to talk things over. You can feel the weight pressing down on your shoulders as the time of the meet gets closer and closer. Do you even know why you want to leave? Can you articulate what's truly bothering you? Do you have any idea of what you would rather do? Let me tell you one thing, your boss definitely doesn't know! Think about how awkward and useless the conversation will be if you do zero preparation.

Don't Waste Time

As you clarify internally what you want and develop your North Star, it becomes easier to determine if a new opportunity isn't going to align with your path. One of my biggest time-wasting moments came when I continued to arrange interviews even though I didn't really want the position I'd applied for. My mindset was, *let's just see how this goes.* Unfortunately, each one of those instances turned out to be a huge waste of my time and other people's time. If you're speaking with an employer and realize you don't want the job, cut it off.

Be Honest with Leverage

A crucial conversation that every developer can relate to is the salary negotiation. A fifteen-minute conversation with a hiring manager will decide what hits your bank account for at least a year.

To prepare for these conversations, be objective about what you bring to the table. The circumstances will be different per conversation— sometimes you will have leverage, other times you won't. The worst thing you can do is over-represent yourself. For example, many developers I've spoken with ask for above-average compensations but don't have the track records to back it up. Software developers make assumptions about what they should be earning just because Glassdoor says so or because they have friends making the big bucks in similar roles. Averages can be helpful guidelines, but you will only be compensated based on your value and what you negotiate for—not based on what other people negotiate for.

To drive the point home again, be honest about your value. Leverage comes with value, and value takes a long time to accumulate. The only place where you can stretch a little is when you set the expectation for the future; sometimes you can sell your employer on your impact in the years to come. This is a sign of good-will from both parties and will pay future dividends if you deliver on those expectations.

What Other People Want

We've established that knowing what you want is priority number one. Discovering what your counterparty wants is priority number two. Consider this as two sides to one coin. When everybody around the table is aware of what everybody else wants, then you can all move forward together. You need to align your needs with your counterparty's in order to arrive at an agreeable position together. Again, this sounds selfish—but it is not. These are merely the mechanisms to have successful conversations.

For example, let's imagine that you feel like you must make a set amount of money per year, no matter what it takes. You've internalized this. This salary must be met. You've prioritized it over the inconvenient commute, the underwhelming work, and a couple questionable interviewer personalities. As a quick aside, I will caution against prioritizing something so strongly at the expense of other factors. If money is truly the deal-breaker for you, your first line of defense should be to not waste time. For example, your target number is probably a financial impossibility for the recently-funded startup. Thus, your effort should be spent targeting medium to large-sized companies that can actually make that number happen.

But what happens if you've exhausted your leads and find yourself negotiating with a tiny startup? Your mind is still prioritizing cash. You know the compensation conversation is going to be hard. First, you must diagnose your counterparty's thoughts so that you can keep their mind open. What does a startup CEO really want? She wants to hire a great developer, pay as little as possible, and get her dream off the ground. You must focus your attention on what she wants. You address her priorities first—you are a great developer, love the mission, and want to put all your energy into shipping code. Don't think of it as keeping her open to salary leeway; it's about keeping her mind open, period.

If you're not careful, your counterparty will easily become combative and go into defensive mode—then you will *definitely not* get what you want. For example, how do you think the conversation will go if you bring up your salary number right out of the gate? Again, what does a startup CEO want? She really doesn't want to burn through all her cash reserves! By not being cognizant of what she wants, you'll completely close off her mind and consequently fail to achieve your salary goal.

When you have proved that you can provide what she wants, you can come back around and discuss money at the tail-end of the conversation:

> "I understand your mission and I know I can ship this thing on budget and within six months. To do this comfortably and consistently for you now and into the future, I would need to have my salary raised. Would you be open to discussing that?"

Conclusion

At the start of my career, I didn't have a clue about this concept. Conversations came and went, and I would think nothing of them. After a few years in the workplace, I noticed that I would never feel positive after having a serious conversation. I was never prepared. I wasn't clear about what I wanted for myself, let alone what the people I was talking to wanted. I kept having unproductive interactions with important people. The conversation would never push me—or the other person—in a better direction.

In the past few years, I have put in significant effort to become vigilantly conscious of these interactions. I look forward to them, I prepare for them, and I strive to grow from them. There are many more crucial conversations to come for both of us; if you haven't started thinking about them, get thinking now!

7: Think Beyond The Ticket [Coding]

Tickets—also known as tasks, issues, or stories—are a regular part of developer life. As of today, the Australians are still dominating ticket management software with JIRA and the Atlassian fleet. For tiny teams, tickets might be an unneeded overhead, but for many companies, *all* your work is tracked with tickets. This ranges from bug fixes, to writing documentation, to designing new architectures.

If getting assigned only one flavor of backlogged tickets comprises one hundred percent of your day, it may be time to ruminate about your job. Software development is not about fixing bugs 24/7. As a developer, there will be a never-ending queue of tickets, but this is not a bad thing. There needs to be a system to organize and track allocated tasks. A lot is said through tickets; let's get ourselves into the right mindset to tackle them.

Hold a Standard

Hold all ticket-creators accountable. If it's a UI touch-up on the settings screen, make sure the designer has attached all the relevant assets. If customer service reports a bug, they must provide steps to reproduce the broken behavior. If you're filing a ticket to your colleague, it better be a step-by-step work of art. Reject any ticket that isn't up to snuff; incomplete context is a waste of your time. Assuming the ticket is on point, clicking the "Accept" button kicks your job into gear. Someone has created a thoughtful ticket, and you will deliver a thoughtful solution.

Don't Be a Robot

Regardless of how thorough the ticket description is, there is always more than meets the eye. Do not perform the bare minimum to resolve the issue; adding one extra else/if clause probably isn't going to cut it. We must always understand the *why* behind our assignments. Who is the stakeholder and why does it matter to him or her? What kind of technical debt led up to this? Is it an innocent bug or something that turns our whole design upside down?

Do not blindly accept and execute tickets at face value—we are not machines. When tackling tickets, understand the *why*, have dialogues with the other stakeholders, and explore the edges. I guarantee everyone involved will appreciate it.

Every Edge Case

Enumerate every edge case. If you're fixing a bug, the ticket will report only one of many scenarios where the problem manifests. Where are the others? Edge cases can also exist outside the context of code. Train yourself to think about edge cases in terms of the whole product or service—I call these the "Business Edge Cases." If the designer has you implementing a new animation for the onboarding flow, maybe it clashes with an animation they had you work on for the checkout page. Bring that up; it could have slipped their mind. Keep an eye out for both technical and non-technical edge cases.

Parallel Awareness

A software team will be tackling a shared pool of tickets. Always be cognizant of what is happening around you. If you're working on a task, how does your work affect your colleagues? Does it help someone out? Does it make their life harder? Is someone else working code that overlaps with this ticket? Can you leverage anything in progress? It's easy to run with a ticket as a walled-off unit of work, but it inevitably leads to divergent implementations and duplicated work without proper communication. Few people have this level of awareness.

Always be cognizant of what is happening around you.

The Whole System

Always consider the entire software system. If the fix is truly a one-liner—that's awesome. If not, ask yourself, *How can I fix this and improve the system at the same time?* Tickets are preliminary indicators of vulnerabilities in your code; use them to preemptively target, learn about, and fix weak areas.

Your Personal Queue

A ticket is just the tip of the iceberg. Every ticket symbolizes much more than a singular piece of work. A low-value developer will take each ticket at face value. A high-value developer uses the ticket to gain awareness of the system as a whole. Fixing the bug is just a nice side-effect.

> *No one else understands the intricacies of the code like we do and it's our responsibility to continually improve it.*

Routinely create tickets for yourself. This doesn't have to be officially sanctioned JIRA tickets stamped by management. This could be your personal to-do list that's scribbled on your notebook. Remember, the non-technical ticket queue will never end, but who's replenishing the technical one? We are. No one else understands the intricacies of the code like we do and it's our responsibility to continually improve it.

Crunch Periods

Tickets are a reflection of work and are subject to a wide range of situations. The above points cover the majority of scenarios, but there will always be fire-fights and crunch periods when tickets won't be created as works of art. For example, if the team is getting ready to launch a big feature at the end of the month, QA might come back with an avalanche of visual problems. It's probably not reasonable to ask for a thorough description and annotated screen capture for all these issues. During times like these, tickets should be triaged quickly and fixed promptly to unblock the big launch.

Conclusion

Take full responsibility for your tickets. If the scope changes, communicate the differential to any stakeholder ASAP. Hold your colleagues accountable and make sure you have the context you need. Hold yourself accountable and make sure your team knows the true nature of your progress. Think thoughtfully about every ticket you tackle and you will become a better software developer.

8: Choosing Your Words [Daily Life]

Every software developer communicates differently. At one end of the spectrum, we have the introverted unicorn developers receiving tasks in small envelopes passed under the door. At the other end, we have the outspoken developers who insist on sharing their opinion with everyone. Software jobs require varying levels of communication. While it might be acceptable to stay quiet in an academic environment, communication skills become a deal-breaker when you work alongside non-technical colleagues—the unicorn might break down after having to sit in a two-hour business requirements meeting.

> *While it might be acceptable to stay quiet in an academic environment, communication skills become a deal-breaker when you work alongside non-technical colleagues*

For software development—as with any other technical discipline—it is imperative that we use the correct language in the correct setting. Thread vs. Process, Concurrency vs. Parallelism, etc. When we use the right language, our colleagues immediately understand what we're talking about. If your co-worker is misusing a word, correct him or her and ask them to return the favor. Choosing the right words is extremely important from both a technical and non-technical perspective.

The Technical Context

From the technical perspective, choosing the right words at the right time can be tricky. One reason this is difficult is because we often jump from one technical context to another as we talk. This context switching becomes more natural as you gain experience, but it can be jarring if you're learning many new words for the first time. Let's talk through four of these so-called technical contexts: system-level, programming languages, third-parties, and your own applications.

When I say system-level, I am referring to anything that is a part of the operating system, raw computer, or distributed network. Abstractly, this is the hardware, or more colloquially, *what* our software is running on. As an aside, remember that the operating system *is not* really hardware. However, for most of us non-kernel developers, the OS is magical enough that we can refer to it just as hardware. That previous sentence is cringe-worthy for many readers, but I hope you catch my drift. Anyways, when you're working in Linux there is a standard set of words and phrases that everyone has agreed upon. Your home directory is always your home directory. Generic-sounding words—process, group permission, scheduling—all have well-defined meanings within the language of Linux. Similarly, latency

If you decide to jump from Ruby over to Python over to Javascript, the word module can take on many different meanings.

and bandwidth have special meanings when you talk about networks. Be careful, these exact words will reappear and be re-used in totally different contexts, but you should know exactly what they mean down at the system level.

Moving past the system level, what about the different programming languages? We use programming languages to describe business logic and model complex systems. For any language, respect its norms and constructs. This can be hard to master when you're jumping from language to language. For example, don't call your Ruby module an abstract interface, just call it what it is—a Ruby module. If you decide to jump from Ruby over to Python over to Javascript, the word module can take on many different meanings. It's easy to interpolate one language's constructs into another, so be careful not to make any cursory assumptions. Presuming that your Java generics are exactly the same as C++ templates, and continuing to call them template classes in Java is exactly the kind of mistake that can cause communication problems. Use the correct words in the right language context.

What about the external libraries and third-party services we don't control? You will encounter generic words such as worker, controller, manager, scheduler, or foobar when working with someone else's code. These nondescript words will have different definitions across different libraries, and no one can be expected to just understand them. To mitigate any confusion, strive to thoroughly understand the libraries, then use prefixes where necessary to clear up any confusion. This is equivalent to real life name-spacing:

"Oh, that code is in the Rails Controller."

"How many Celery Workers are we running on that computer?"

Last but not least, you will create your own application-specific words for your own project. For effective communication, make sure the team is at a consensus on how things are named. If your team hasn't developed a naming convention, bring it up and define whatever needs to be defined. During the next group sync-up, if your colleague says, "We need to refactor our secondary-layer arbiter orchestration meta classes!" everyone should know exactly what's going on—even if the words themselves are ridiculous.

The Non-Technical Context

Within the organization, there will be business-specific words that the company will develop over time. These will be absurd names and acronyms that turn into normal company lingo. Despite the absurdity, these words must still be navigated and used consistently to make everyone's life easier.

At a previous job, I spent a lot of time developing custom Customer Relationship Management (CRM) software and internal tooling. Every company can fire up Salesforce and track customers, but once you inject a

CRM with industry-specific knowledge, things start to get complicated—modeling hospital patients is very different than modeling real-estate leads. The way an operator

This layer is crucial and turns into the shared, non-technical, company language.

thinks about his or her industry is not going to match one-to-one with how you decide to implement your software. An internal business layer must be established between you and the industry experts. This layer is crucial and turns into the shared, non-technical, company language. Good operators will know how to translate business requirements to the company language, and you will know exactly how to take that and translate it into code. Take it upon yourself to define this business language.

In software, there is the concept of "overloading"—there is a similar concept at work in business. This happens when the shared company language is not well defined and one word begins to take on multiple meanings. Even worse than this, there may be holes in the language, causing communication breakdowns between business and technology. This is all part of the non-technical context that you must pay attention to! Develop this language with your colleagues and it will facilitate effective communication across all departments. The business guys may not acknowledge the problem, but you—the clear-thinking developer—will step up and *define* what needs to be defined. Everyone wins.

Precision

The right words at the right time facilitate precise descriptions. A sales pitch by its very nature can be fluffy and poetic, but a technical solution off the back of a direct question must be short and to the point.

Conclusion

Any situation—technical or non-technical—benefits from concise language. Use language that befits the context and the audience. When you get this right, your audience will automatically align on the same wavelength, as everything is understood by everyone. This is a priceless skill and will improve your effectiveness as a developer.

9: Embrace Confusion [Learning]

Tammy was one of the few women in CMU's Electrical and Computer Engineering Class of 2009. She's currently a software developer in Los Angeles and has been my friend for over ten years. I have seen the engineer grow in her year after year. After getting her MS in ECE, Tammy wasn't sold on following through with tech. After a few years of unenthusiastic engineering, Tammy began dipping her toes in digital design. After being unimpressed with the laws of UX, she slowly found her way back to software. This chapter doesn't do full justice to her journey, but it showcases invaluable traits for any engineer.

This is the *third* time I'm taking "Intro to C." This class is old news for my friends and I desperately need to get through it. Third time's the charm, right?

The first lecture isn't bad—Introduction to the Syllabus. *I got this.* The second week rolls around and we get our first lab assignment. It's something to do with pointers and I just don't get it. *It's ok.* I fight my initial impulse to flee and stick with it. I don't exactly know how to start, but it's not due just yet, so I still have some time. By the third week of class, the professor has moved on to a more complex topic, something to do with linked lists. What does a pointer dereference mean again? Do all intro classes move this fast, or am I really that slow? I have to digest pointers, finish the first lab, and keep up with all these new lectures.

I drop the class.

For the third time.

I'd found myself enrolled in CMU's ECE program almost by surprise. I wasn't die-hard about computers in high school, but it was a respectable school and a respectable field—definitely good enough for any 17-year-old. I knew it was going to be hard, but I didn't think it would be *that* hard.

> I knew it was going to be hard, but I didn't think it would be *that* hard.

During the program, I felt isolated in my discouragement. I felt as if I was the only one who didn't understand the lectures, the only one who struggled with the labs. Later in life, I would come to realize that these feelings were very, very normal. I'm very proud of my CMU degree, but at the same time I know I could have pushed myself harder. I spent five years staying relatively comfortable by avoiding some of the really challenging— AKA rewarding—classes.

After school ended, I slowly and steadily upgraded my mindset and changed my learning strategy. Here, I want to share a few important points that I've learned since obtaining my degree.

Dealing with Confusion

Every engineering discipline comes with its fair share of confusion. Programming can be enjoyable, but everyone goes through some late nights banging their head against the wall debugging. How you deal with this mind-numbing confusion is what's most important.

Ever since I was elementary school, I've always enjoyed repetitive math problems. I could sit there and do multiplication and long division for hours. I knew what I was doing; I felt in control. This carried over into high

> *Despite the discomfort, you must step up and embrace confusion.*

school—algebra, trigonometry, calculus—it was all easy. The cakewalk ended the moment I stepped into university-level engineering.

All of a sudden, every assignment was open-ended. The professor gave us a few introductory lectures and set us loose on challenging coding labs. For me, I was not accustomed to this level of confusion. This wasn't multiplication and algebra. I felt intimated, lost, not in control. I didn't like it.

Over many years of working and being independent, I've slowly learned how to handle these feelings of confusion. Despite the discomfort, you must step up and *embrace* confusion. Many people underestimate this mindset. It's not something that comes naturally, but it can be learned. This is an essential attitude for any engineering discipline.

Everyone Feels Discouraged—It's Done on Purpose

I was not alone in my discouragement at CMU. The curriculum took a toll on everyone and I never realized the amount of extra time everyone put in just to stay afloat until much later.

For many engineering curriculums, the courses are purposefully designed to overwhelm you. The lectures move like lightning, the labs are intense, and you *will* fall behind. On top of this, the school instills a feverish sense of competitiveness among its students. You're competing for the top scores in every class, the coolest internships, and the biggest job offers. To top it all off, whatever energy you have left goes into appearing competent in front of your peers. The atmosphere weighs heavily on every student.

If you're feeling discouraged, I guarantee that your peers share similar feelings. *Do not assume you are alone.* Talk openly with other people, try to help each other, and never feel embarrassed about your own progress. If someone judges you by that, they are not worth your time.

You Have to Put in the Work

This is the most clichéd thing that can be said, but it must be said—you have to put a lot of work in! Putting in the work was a value I developed after embarking on my professional career. This was a natural evolution from what I call my old "just enough" mentality. Being exposed to a concept via a lecture and completing the homework isn't going to cut it. Copying a piece of code and massaging it into a feature isn't good enough. You have to go the extra mile and put in those hours. It's the only way to get true value out of your learning.

When I got deeper into software as a professional, I started taking tons of online courses to supplement my knowledge. I offered to build free websites for my friends just to practice my coding. I became pro-active and left my comfort zone often. Sometimes I wish I had developed this mindset earlier in my life—I think my peers already had it in college—but I'm extremely grateful to have it now.

Thoughtful Questions

As developers, we must be comfortable independently digging for information. An awesome byproduct of doing your own research and reading instruction manuals is that you begin to ask more thoughtful questions.

If you provide a thoughtful question, you will get a thoughtful answer.

I've been blessed with the opportunity to work with extremely generous co-workers. I'm eternally grateful to them for spending their valuable time teaching me. To do my part, I always do my homework and come prepared with thoughtful questions.

"How does XYZ work?" is *not* a thoughtful question. It shows that you haven't independently researched or dug for anything. This is a better question:

"I see that we built XYZ for customer request ABC. Why did we choose to use the FOO pattern for XYZ? Have we considered doing it using the MOO pattern?"

If you provide a thoughtful question, you will get a thoughtful answer. Other people's time is precious—as is yours—so make sure you get the best out of it. Do your research, spend some time developing your questions, and don't ask the same one twice!

Conclusion

The secret sauce for me has always been this simple idea—embracing confusion. During college, confusion caused me to feel intimidated, drop out of classes, and hold back with my studies. In my professional life, embracing confusion has steadily pushed me across disciplines and roles. At my current company, I started off as an entry-level product designer helping design banners, logos, and other marketing assets. Even though the work was enjoyable, there was always that small string leading back to coding waiting to be pulled. This mindset—mixed in with some consistent work and thoughtful questions—has enabled me to keep pulling that string and building my career.

We must be very comfortable being uncomfortable. When that level of comfort is our norm, challenges and foreign topics become enjoyable—dare I say fun—to encounter and take on.

10: Digging Yourself Out Of Demotivation [Career]

In the following story, Ross recounts his years writing software at a large consulting company. It showcases common forms of demotivation and, more importantly, provides methods to push through negativity. Every one of us can relate to the uninspiring hours writing code we don't want to write. Ross's story shows that there is always something you can do about it.

Demotivation is a subtle process. One day you're honeymooning with a company, and the very next day you suddenly hate looking at the code. What just happened?

My first job out of school was with a consulting company. Ironically, this came after calling nonsense on consulting ever since I was a freshman. During fall semesters, companies would come give workshops about their new-graduate positions. These were excellent sources of free pizza and also mildly educational insomuch as they told you all about the different opportunities out there for new engineers. The consulting companies were the worst; the number of "synergies" and "fully-integrated solutions" mentioned made me want to flip tables. My freshman self would have scoffed at my senior self, but a job's a job.

In a consulting company, projects come and go. Management sells this as a constant stream of challenging work:

"Nothing is ever stale!"

"You get to work with <Insert Forbes 500 Company>!"

"You'll be solving a diverse set of problems!"

It's a great sell, but my colleagues and I quickly developed a very different sentiment.

I was only two projects in and my motivation had already begun to fade. I felt hopelessly detached from my work. Management wasn't lying—nothing was ever stale, and that was the problem. We had built nothing for ourselves. We had zero technical identity. When you take on a contract, everything you create eventually gets handed over to the client. It's their product, or problem, after you're done with it. I found myself in a brand-new code base every six months, with a severe lack of pride in any of my work. A lack of recognizable ownership is a particularly dangerous feeling for any software developer.

Let's do a quick summary of the company dynamic. On the ground, there are a ton of software developer teams. Each team is given one big client project at a time. Every project has one, maybe two, business

> *We had built nothing for ourselves. We had zero technical identity.*

analysts. This role has recently won the award for "Most Generic Sounding Title of All Time."

In the beginning, I underestimated the business analysts, but over time, I came to greatly admire them. It's an extremely important and difficult role. These were the people who spoke directly to the clients and gathered all the information on each and every job. It's a very simple job description, but not so simple when it comes to execution. They consider all the clients' requirements and spec out the systems at an extremely high level. What are the inputs? Outputs? Edge cases over here, edge cases over there. Finally, they communicate all of that to us—the developers.

To round this out, we had project managers who would oversee a handful of projects. They would schedule meetings and make sure things were staying on track. Their main objective was to keep the software progressing and make sure the business analysts were staying on-point with the client requirements. I always considered these as glorified meeting schedulers, but, again, they played an *extremely* valuable role; without them, projects would fall apart.

After I'd worked on three or four projects, the seeds of my demotivation had rooted themselves. I wasn't in control over any of my work. I had no freedom of choice, from which projects I worked on, all the way down to the features I was implementing. Since developers never spoke with the clients, the main creators and delegators of work were always the business analysts. It felt like a big game of telephone.

As a result, life became a never-ending queue of JIRA tickets. These tickets were

> *We didn't know **why** we were working on these tickets, but we **had** to work on them.*

supposed to map to real requirements, but you can only take things at face value for so long. For me, this was the essence of my demotivation. We didn't know *why* we were working on these tickets, but we *had* to work on them. I knew that in some meeting room somewhere, a conversation was being held about what the engineers should be spending their time on, but that was a conversation I was never a part of.

I would like to tell you that I personally turned a new leaf and became a happier developer. Unfortunately, that's not the story. Everything changed when a new developer, Jennifer, joined our team. She single-handedly lifted our team into a better place. Her actions and attitude were exemplary, and I hope they motivate you like they motivated me.

First, Jenn came in with raw curiosity—a feeling we had all lost long ago. She didn't mind our never-ending queue of tickets. She would pick up the most mundane ticket and run with it. She asked thoughtful questions and dived into code that no one else wanted to touch.

At this point, I admit that I wasn't the happiest camper. My colleagues and I were doing the bare minimum to meet our business analysts' requirements. We were long past the most important part of software development—caring. When an eager new graduate asks you why you implemented a particular feature the way you did, it's embarrassing to admit that you got lazy. Jenn made us start caring again.

Jenn quickly surpassed all her peers in value. About a year into the job, she started venturing into uncharted territory—customer meetings. We realized that if we wanted to sit in on customer meetings, all we had to do was ask. I guess we had been too busy complaining to try! Jenn started attending these meetings, growing relationships with customers, and what started out as quiet observation turned into something much, much more.

This was a win-win-win situation for us. Clients who were growing tired of our business analysts complacently nodding to their demands now had a person they could have a real back-and-forth discussion with. Since Jenn knew the intricacies behind the implementations, she was able to thoroughly and transparently respond to customers.

I cannot stress how much they appreciated this. Our status quo of black box communication in the company had been disrupted. Jenn's interaction with customers turned into model behavior for the entire company. To get on her level, other business analysts had to put in extra time to understand the tech and be ready to give Jenn-level answers to our customers' probing questions.

To complete the triple-play win, Jenn's model interaction was a breath of fresh air for the developers. As requirements cleared up and became reasonable, we started to care more and more about our work. Nebulous tickets with generic descriptions were replaced with focused milestones

The key to unlock all doors is always communication.

where everyone understood the *why*. Once you get everyone on the same page of *why*, the *how* turns out to be pretty easy. I wasn't lying when I said a single person lifted our whole team up!

The key to unlock all doors is always communication. Before Jenn stepped up, we were isolated and undeservingly grumpy in our dark developer caves. I didn't fully appreciate communication until I saw its value through Jenn. She knew all the code, knew all the business requirements, and seamlessly transitioned between the two.

If you feel like you're wallowing in demotivation, remember that you are in more control of your attitude than you think; there *is* something that you can do, and it starts with communication. Don't stay too long in the grumpy developer cave, don't wait for a Jenn to come by to motivate you, and don't underestimate how much control you have over your own mindset.

11: Speaking At Meetings [Daily Life]

Meetings are a universal part of every job and contribute significantly to your personal brand within the company. As an introverted engineer, pursuing any kind of presence in team meetings has never come naturally to me, but I have come to appreciate its importance. Whether you like it or not, your personal brand will directly affect your experience in any corporate setting. Meetings develop your brand, and they must be navigated.

Don't Speak Right Away

Unless you are the host, there's no need to be the first one to speak in a meeting. As an attendee, focus on the meeting's theme, and get a feel for the mood. What is the current collective state of mind? There is no point speaking up if you have no idea what anyone is thinking—pay attention.

> *Whether you like it or not, your personal brand will directly affect your experience in any corporate setting.*

Who's in the room, who's listening, and from what position are they participating? The VP is dropping in and just wants a quick overview—no need for nitty-gritty details. Your manager's ass is on the line and he's sweating over the new roadmap—give a detailed progress report. The grumpy senior engineer is upset because the team didn't follow through with their proposed design—let's not pour any more salt on that wound.

As the meeting progresses, get as much of a feel for the mood as you can. This shouldn't take long if you're perceptive and stay focused—you will have Jedi mind-tricks soon.

Learn Everyone's Personality

People's current state of mind is fickle; you must go deeper and understand their core personalities. This will take some time, but the knowledge is crucial for the long-term and will improve all future interactions you have with your colleagues.

Understanding the foundation of your coworkers' personalities allows for seamless communication with them. What's their basic behavior? Some people love to hear their own voice, so let them air their thoughts. Other people love to

> *Understanding the foundation of your coworkers' personalities allows for seamless communication with them.*

be disapprovingly silent; pull them into the conversation with guiding questions. How do your colleagues prefer to digest information? Some people understand things through numbers, others through stories, and others through logic. Gather every single nuance you can from everyone around you, and do it discreetly.

Understand People's Expertise

Understand where everyone's expertise lies and what they do. Big company or small company, you will be in meetings with a recurring set of people. If you're ever in the dark, research the meeting participants ahead of time and find out what they work on. Dig into their projects, their background, and what frameworks they've been using. It will empower you to have this information on hand, as you will know exactly what the other people are bringing to the table.

> *During a meeting, ideas build on each other and you need to be on top—ideally ahead—of the group's train of thought.*

Focus

Maintain focus throughout meetings and follow the group's train of thought. It is easy to let your mind wander. Bring a notebook and scribble down notes on everything, whether it seems important at the time or not. You can flesh them out later. When you get your footing, focus hard on what is being said. During a meeting, ideas build on each other and you need to be on top—ideally ahead—of the group's train of thought.

Give and Receive Credit

There is only so much thunder to go around. Someone will steal yours, just as you will take another's. If you're not cognizant of this, you can easily find yourself in someone's bad graces.

Give credit where credit is due. For example, let's say that you've been working with Sarah on a feature for the past three months. During a status meeting, you get called upon to give a status report. If you give the report as if you've done everything, you become the jerk thunder-taker—don't do this. The words you choose are essential:

> "Sarah and I had a few good design meetings, and *we* came to the conclusion that we shouldn't use Google APIs for this feature anymore."

The *we* is critical. Try replacing it with *I* and see how bad it sounds. Acknowledgments live and die through the use of simple words.

What about the thunder stolen from you? While some may not care for such things, you have the right to expect your dues. If this happens repeatedly, approach Sarah amicably.

> "Sarah, I would appreciate it if you could mention that we both contributed to the project when you give your status updates."

Psychology + Body Language

Read up on basic human psychology and try to become aware of body language. These are basic life skills, abilities that come with time for everyone, but they're worth working on—in a meeting, being able to read the room is a noteworthy skill.

When You Don't Know the Answer

On those (hopefully) rare occasions when you have the spotlight but no idea what to do or say, the best option is to admit that you don't have the answer. Right afterwards, communicate to everyone that you intend to follow up on the issue and provide a thorough update later. It can be as simple as saying you'll look into it. Show that you take every question seriously and will give it attention.

12: Code Sense [Coding]

As a software-naïve college junior, I landed an onsite interview with an advertising company in New York City. The job was 100% web programming and I had 0% experience with web code. My expectations were minimal—let's get through this interview without too much embarrassment and enjoy an all-expenses-paid trip to NYC for the weekend. To my surprise, the internship bar was pretty low, and I passed the interviews with some pre-meditated definitions of encapsulation and polymorphism. I got an offer and took the job.

Despite my best efforts, I was an extremely confused intern; I had no idea what was going on. I spent that summer monkey coding my way into productivity. Monkey coding is when you copy and paste other pieces of code and carefully massage it to do what you want. For huge code bases, this gets you by and requires minimal knowledge of how things are actually working. I had a few recurring thoughts during my time there:

> *I can't believe I'm allowed to contribute to the codebase. Shouldn't there be some   auditing or something?*

> *I really didn't understand that environment setup.*

> *This seems like a terrible way to implement this, but I'm too much of a noob to propose anything better—this doesn't feel good.*

> *I spent that summer monkey coding my way into productivity.*

Despite my unrest, I still had a productive summer. I learned basic web development, wrote some Java, played with SQL, and pushed out a handful of useful features for the company. We even won an internship project challenge just for having a good presentation. All in all, it was a solid eleven weeks.

That summer was significant for me; I discovered that I severely *lacked* something. I trampled my way through rampant hacks and poor design, and I couldn't do anything about it. I got things working, but never felt like I really developed it. I was missing something—the elusive "code sense." This sixth sense comes with time, and it's something we as software developers are constantly developing. It's the first impression you get when you look at a file. It's the ability to spot bottlenecks and pinpoint vulnerabilities early. It's being able to thoroughly fix a bug once and for all. It's avoiding nonsensical dependencies, recognizing subtle side effects, and much, much more.

Where does your code sense originate from? It comes from writing a lot of code and being conscious of its quality. The more code you write, the cleaner it becomes and the more code sense you accumulate. Here are some of my top points for clean code.

Leave Code Cleaner Than You Found It

Every piece of code can perpetually be improved upon. If you see a subtle inconsistency, fix it. If you can't fix it, question it. This creates a virtuous cycle where everything—from a local variable name to a complex code path—slowly improves.

The alternative is that the source tree doesn't get any water. This is the road that leads to a convoluted and frustrating codebase. This is the road that leads to those inevitable complaints you'll hear from developer friends:

> "Our code base sucks! The people who wrote this were so incompetent!"

Let's be honest with ourselves, whose fault is it when the code base sucks?

There's an important caveat to all this. You must only change code that *actually* needs to be changed. If it's not broken, don't fix it. This year, Blizzard announced that they're rebooting StarCraft with some visual touch-ups, but they stated explicitly that they wouldn't touch anything to do with gameplay. If you can get a project to this level, congratulations. For the rest of us, your code will constantly be in flux and demand change—it needs to be taken care of. Some call this the "Boy Scout Rule."

You must only change code that actually needs to be changed. If it's not broken, don't fix it.

Recognize When Things Get Hard to Change

Clean code is flexible and can easily be updated. You don't measure software in terms of it being complete or incomplete, you measure it in terms of how well it can withstand change. It's a bad sign when a simple feature addition feels like you have to rebuild the Death Star.

Major companies have seen their products fall into obscurity through convoluted software. Unless you're Google and swim in Scrooge McDuck vaults of gold, the universal rule of "time is money" applies to all software development. As a developer, you are responsible for your company's code. If the team can't complete their tasks within a reasonable amount of time, then the software is doing the business a disservice and money will be lost. Always keep an eye on the deadline. Ease of change and overall flexibility are great code health checks.

Readability

Many developers—yourself included—will read your code in the future. In one year, I guarantee that you will forget about the classes you wrote this past week. For sanity's sake, optimize for readability. You are writing software for the future; never underestimate how long your code will stick around in the source.

Focus on flow, be deliberate with comments, try to keep files under a thousand lines, and don't get lazy with formatting. Everyone can learn to deal with a condensed coding style and fancy language techniques, but no one can uncover what was on your mind when you put that hack in.

Consistent and Thoughtful Naming Conventions

Naming is simultaneously the easiest and hardest part of programming. Put in your utmost to name things consistently and thoughtfully. Do not break existing convention due to personal preference, do not blindly copy-paste, and do not declare variables with single-character names.

If you've done a good job, your peers will nod their heads quietly through most of your code and be able to focus their feedback on core changes.

Thoughtful naming enables effective communication, which produces happy developers. You will be in endless meetings, code-reviews, and brainstorming sessions. During these gatherings, no one wants to nit-pick over poor naming conventions. Even if there isn't any verbal nit-picking, just seeing someone else's awkward naming can leave a bad taste in your mouth. If you've done a good job, your peers will nod their heads quietly through most of your code and be able to focus their feedback on core changes. Don't underestimate the power of naming and consistency in your code, it will save you and your colleagues precious time and brain energy.

Be Careful with Dependencies

Be careful with dependencies! This is much easier said than done. If one of your micro-services is heavily catered towards every application it serves, it's not a very useful service. If two or more objects in the system always rely on each other, ask yourself: *Can these things ever exist separately? Should they just be one thing?* Thoughtless dependencies beget technical debt. We must stay vigilant.

Life becomes simpler with one-way dependencies. They work on many levels, but let's take a look at a high-level example: third party libraries. You add in a one-liner and get some useful functionality pumped into your project—almost like video game cheat codes. If you've done a good job as the third-party author, you will have clear documentation, an intuitive interface, and a seamless integration process for any client to use your code—this is how you get those GitHub stars. There are countless high-caliber projects out there, but for some reason we seldom have that level of detail with our own code.

My last point is about dependency injection—don't abuse it. This feature is magical and convenient, but it doesn't mean you can start making everything available everywhere. Having one hundred parameters in your constructor, or fifty auto-wired private variables, can be extremely convenient, but it still isn't a good look. Dependency injection makes life easier, but at the end of the day, it's still a dependency.

Keep dependencies at the forefront of your thinking. If the machinery in your system is too tightly coupled, the smallest change will have a huge ripple effect and you'll be cursing the moment you attempt to fix that deceptively innocent-looking bug.

Organization at All Levels

Enforce stringent organization on every level. Here are three levels as a rough guide. First, the raw software must be clean. Use design patterns as long as they make sense and refrain from introducing fancy new ones for "fun." Second, the directory and file structure must be intuitive and consistent—here is where we keep third-party libraries, this is where our schema definitions go, and here is how you separate versioned interface files. Third, put effort into building and deploying. How clean is our build process? Artifacts always go here, documentation always gets generated there, and the version number always gets updated like this.

Every level of software development needs this level of attention. Starting with individual lines of code, this detailed attention should go all the way up to how you finally deploy out to production—the whole system should stay highly organized.

Show That You Care

All code will always reflect the code writer's commitment. How do you personally develop a baseline for this? You start by practicing this commitment yourself. We must care about the code we write—it is our craft.

There are two benefits here. First, your baseline as a developer rises—you will writer better code, faster. Second, you will naturally recognize sloppy code and your code sense will strengthen. Your attention to detail is what sets you apart.

Conclusion

We're just at the tip of the iceberg here. There are awesome books out there on how to write clean code and be a great software developer. Learn more than one language, try out new frameworks, and keep your queue of reading materials fresh. Always care about the code you write, write a lot of it, and you'll get your own magical code sense in no time.

13: Does Going To A Good School Matter? [Learning]

This question is ranked #3 on my list of most popular FAQs. As careers in software development continue to trend, there are now numerous ways to get your foot in the door. The classical way is entering higher education, pursuing a four-year college degree, and entering the workforce post-graduation.

In addition to this, we now have accelerated boot camps that train productive developers in six months and send them off to big tech companies. I can personally attest to their results, having seen an acquaintance go from zero coding to Uber developer within one year—quite incredible. Yet another new entry method is the gradual cross-departmental transition, supported by large companies. A friend of mine started his career as a customer support representative, transitioned into a manual quality assurance (QA) role, and eventually got a position as a developer—all at the same company.

With so many different entry points and backgrounds, the tendency for comparison arises. Developers from boot camps want to know how they stack up against the MIT graduate working beside them. High school grads begin to debate whether or not it's a good idea to invest the heavy cash to get their bachelor's when they see boot camp graduates getting six figures after six months. So—does going to a good school matter?

The advantages that academia provides can be wildly different. Some will say it was the perfect springboard into their careers, and others will question if there were any advantages at all. I was lucky enough to gain a lot out of my years at Carnegie Mellon. Everyone's situation will be different and it's impossible for me to determine if going to a good school matters for you specifically. Many variables play into what you get out of school. For me personally, it *definitely* mattered, and here was my circumstance.

First, I am fortunate enough to have been provided the resources to attend university. My parents grew up during the Cultural Revolution and were forcefully removed from academics to go work in the countryside. After it ended, they picked up their studies, moved to America, and saved enough money to send me to an absurdly priced private school. They have my eternal gratitude and I will be hard-pressed to follow their achievements.

Second, I targeted my major of choice while I was still in high school. After years of gaming, building computers, and taking introductory C courses, I had an affinity towards engineering. I wasn't exactly making a ten-year plan as a high school junior, but I had made up my mind about what to study. I applied early decision to CMU, got in, and that was it. I mention this because it's uncommon to be so definitive about higher academics when you're 16. Many of my friends had trouble deciding what to study and fell into generic majors. Some flip-flopped between colleges; others found themselves with degrees that they weren't quite sure what to do with.

Third, I was able to participate in a world-class engineering program. I will enumerate a few of the benefits, but there are many more than this. The professors are the top of their fields and have honed their textbooks and curriculums over decades. Challenging course work and peer-to-peer competition instill strong work ethic into students—a skill that translates beyond coding. The school has a huge network and goes above and beyond to set students up for their first jobs. This includes frequent job fairs, round-the-clock career centers, and an up-to-date alumni directory. Overall, the institution provides a lot.

My story sounds like the perfect, classical entry point into tech—and it was. I solidly hit all three criteria. I was lucky enough to have the resources and support from my family, I knew early on what I was going to study, and I was fortunate to be a part of an amazing program. So, for me, the stars did align and going to a good school did matter. However, this is only my circumstance and will be completely different from yours. Perhaps you're only comfortable with two out of three of these criteria points, perhaps you have none of them, or maybe this story is not even remotely relatable for you.

Before jumping into the chapter, I have a few additional introductory points to make. First, if none of the stars align for you, tread with extra caution. If you're indifferent about what to study, are considering taking out debilitating student loans, and didn't get into a strong program—maybe you should think twice about that bachelor's degree. Second, take stock of your responsibilities. If you have dependents, medical bills, and loans to pay, perhaps putting a four-year pause on your life to be a full-time computer science student isn't feasible. Finally, school fills a short period of your life and the knowledge you gain there will be overshadowed by the knowledge gained later. It is not the be-all, end-all of your learning, but merely a place where you have the opportunity to lay your technical foundation.

The Name Counts

We are all judged continuously throughout the entirety of our lives. We are powerless to prevent these judgments, and we're usually just as guilty as the next person of making them. But we *are* empowered to choose how we let judgments affect us—it's not a big deal unless *you* make it a big deal. In the completely subjective and wishy-washy arena of judgment, we must do our best to start with a solid footing.

> We are powerless to prevent these judgments, and we're usually just as guilty as the next person of making them.

External judgment starts with our accomplishments. A childhood spent playing RPGs makes me look at my own accomplishments as badges—You've earned the High School Diploma Badge! +1 Competency! We are judged on everything—the languages and frameworks we've used, the places we've worked, and the schools we've attended. All of these accumulate and their branding *always* counts. Our society revolves around these markers and it's why we still utilize résumés and LinkedIn.

I was working at a large corporation for almost four years before I decided to jump ship and get into start-ups. The transition was difficult because I had none of the skills that the startups I approached actually valued. I had C/C++ on my résumé instead of Ruby on Rails. How could an embedded developer know how to write web applications? No way! The reason—truthfully, the *only* reason—that some startups talked to me was that they saw Carnegie Mellon next to "Education" on my résumé. That single badge was enough to get my foot in the door.

The Work Ethic

Many people underestimate the work ethic gained from a challenging engineering curriculum. This is more than just learning linear algebra, implementing basic algorithms, and understanding how a computer works. These are the habits, mindset, and attitude towards tackling problems. You can gain this in a variety of places. Maybe you learned how to work hard by starting your own T-shirt business in high school. Maybe your work ethic came from years of moonlighting projects after your nine-to-five. A strong work ethic takes time to develop.

> *The mindset and routines behind a strong work ethic must be developed.*

One benefit of academia is that a four-year engineering program will give you this for free. I didn't notice this until I became a professional. I realized I had gained much more than just book knowledge; repeatedly spending eight hours in a computer lab builds out some grit.

The mindset and routines behind a strong work ethic must be developed. You can either get this automatically with academic study, or you can grow it in your own way. I include it here because it is a convenient byproduct of a challenging school and it is often overlooked. Learning and working hard is a lifelong process; make this your mindset.

Better School, Better Education

Better schools will provide a better education. There is a reason why MIT is MIT. Elite schools are elite for a reason, and they have honed their curriculums over many years. Not all "Intro to Programming" courses are created equal.

No Shortcuts

Good things come with time. The rise of software boot camps has given people the unrealistic notion that they can become a software developer in the space of three to six months. Boot camps are a result of the market;

the world demands more developers and these camps create the supply.

Boot camps are great entry points into software development, as long as your expectations are realistic. If you have the time and money, an accelerated program might be a great catalyst for your future career. In doing so, however, stay mindful that you are only dipping your toes into the water—there is a long journey ahead of you. To be clear, I am not dismissing boot camps, I've seen a select few that have trained great developers and provide thorough programs. I will issue a warning, though, for *anything* that is advertised as a shortcut—when it sounds too good to be true, it always is.

Structure Helps

When you're a Level 1 Warrior, you will need some structure to get started. At ground zero, you don't even know what you don't know. This is when the core benefit of an academic institution—the curriculum—has huge value.

One of the biggest pain points I've seen with aspiring developers is that they're not sure what to study first, what to study after, and how to fill in the blanks. I have seen exceptions to this, but only among people who have previously experienced structured learning. For example, a previous candidate I interviewed held a PhD in mathematics and was able to pick up programming in a few months with no problems. He had already developed the habits and analytical intuition to steadily progress through coding. If you've been a freelance blog writer since high school, the knowledge path might not be as clear.

With school, this path has been paved for you; all you have to do is put in the work. These roads are not so clear once you leave academia. Whether you choose to go to school or not, I highly recommend using a structured curriculum in the beginning. You will be flying blind and wasting your time otherwise.

Conclusion

Committing to school is a significant decision for anyone. If the circumstances are favorable and your objective is well-defined, I think the full classical four-year degree provides great benefits. However, your situation will be unique and you will have to make your own call. There are countless examples of successful software developers who did not come from the classical approach. Finally, do not forget about the habits and mindset behind a strong work ethic. Whether it's through school or on your own, this value must grow and stay with us for our entire lives.

14: Cross-Disciplinary Assumptions [Daily Life]

I met Billy in San Diego, while he was writing code for a defense contracting company in Los Angeles. Since then, he switched career paths to become a product manager (PM) and now works in New York City. When I asked Billy about his juiciest stories, he prefaced all of them with one major theme—the over-simplification of someone else's work.

As a non-developer, here's the worst thing you can say to a developer:

> "Hey Joe, these new features shouldn't be too hard to implement, right?"

Five years ago, I made the transition from developer to product manager. What is a PM? An easy, but unrealistic, reference point is Steve Jobs. Think about Steve for three seconds—then come back down to reality. A product manager is someone who is able to generate a vision, communicate it to the people that need to implement it, and facilitate its iteration. He or she will understand the customers and uncover their pain points. At an even higher level, the PM will uncover things the customers don't even know they want. A company's revenue and brand are defined by its products. The PM is

A product manager is someone who is able to generate a vision, communicate it to the people that need to implement it, and facilitate its iteration.

the one responsible for managing its development.

The easy part is generating the vision; ideas are cheap. The meat and potatoes of the work revolve around communication and implementation. The scope of product and your responsibility will vary. At an ivory-tower, Steve Jobs level, you dream up the idea of the iRocket and an army of people under you build it. Small startups employ a single PM to create a holistic product, style, and brand for the company. For larger companies, product managers are placed hierarchically, just like any other role. You might be managing a couple new buttons for iTunes, or you could be planning Apple's ten-year roadmap.

Overall, this is a thankless job, and I concede that it is often filled with a healthy amount of baloney. The bottom line for a PM focuses on how well the product is doing, yet this is most likely out of their control. From my experience, responsibilities are split between two themes: research and implementation.

For research, you must dig into analytics, locate the elusive "market fit," and determine how the product integrates into the business. You must study the competition, conduct consumer studies, and make decisions about what should or should not be built. The implementation is trickier because the PM doesn't implement anything. This comes down to getting everyone else on board to deliver and iterate on the product. The day-to-day of this work is nuanced and complex. It revolves around your salesmanship of the product, your communication skills, and the respect you garner from your colleagues. PMs will sway along this spectrum. Some will live in documentation and research, while others will just "get it done." On the surface, this role appears to come with great power, but in reality, it is very much the opposite.

As a PM, I've lost count of the number of heated clashes I've had with developers. Behind ninety-five percent of these situations, the root cause is always the same—we make assumptions about each other's work. The developers tell me what parts of the product need to be cut, and I tell the developers that building out password reset is "no biggie." I attribute many of these fights to me being a developer in my previous life. Cross-disciplinary assumptions are dangerous and can be a surefire way to rub someone the wrong way if you're not careful.

I take great pride in being an ex-coder. It has helped me communicate and empathize with developers; I appreciate their work more than most. My self-proclaimed title of "Technical PM" also has a nice ring to it. After school, I spent two years writing Java at a consulting company. We were fulfilling contracts for huge government projects. It wasn't the sexiest job, but it was a job, and I got a taste of what it meant to sift through millions of lines of code.

After two years of Eclipse grinding and stepping through break-points, I started attending customer meetings out of curiosity. Speaking with customers automatically turned me into the "Requirement Translator" for my fellow developers. Shortly after this, I was given the generic title of "Business Analyst." I did that for about half a year before I picked up my first role as a PM.

Why is my career transition relevant? Because I want to make one point very clear—no matter how technically inclined you think you are, you should never make assumptions about the technical implementations involved in any project. Let's put that even more generally: you should never make assumptions about another person's job. Period.

I can't control your thoughts. I can't stop you from thinking, *God dammit, this developer is lagging. I know this feature isn't too hard!* But I urge you to be careful when these thoughts arise. Thoughts easily leak into actions and subconscious behaviors. While your thoughts will always be your thoughts, your actions affect everyone around you. You must act tactfully to maintain a comfortable work environment for you and your colleagues.

Everything we've talked about so far is what *you* should do. You must keep your assumptions in check, you must act with tact, you must respect the difficulty of someone else's work. But what happens when this comes back around at you? As a PM, I get bombarded with product opinions 24/7. Every single department, from marketing, to design, to engineering, *all* have their own would-be-Steve-Jobs insights.

Originally, for many of my cross-departmental conflicts, I felt justified in making engineering assumptions because the engineers were making product assumptions. If they kept telling me what to change in the product, I could keep telling them which features were easy to implement, right? No, this is the wrong way of thinking. Because someone tells me how to do my job, it doesn't automatically give me the right to tell them how to do theirs.

The core principle that has guided me through these fights is the humble acknowledgement of mutual purpose. Mutual purpose is a mindset that we must steer ourselves towards. It won't be second nature for most. Always remember that you and your colleagues—despite having very different specialties—are working towards the same goals. You're both struggling to get more customers and five-star reviews. You're both on the line

> *The core principle that has guided me through these fights is the humble acknowledgement of mutual purpose.*

to get the project finished on time. In the grand scheme of things, your cross-disciplinary quarrels are dwarfed by the larger goals of the collective. Furthermore, your random issues at work are blips on the radar when you consider your whole life.

For all the developers out there, respect the product managers and designers—let them do their jobs. When cross-departmental issues arise, be tactful in how you communicate, and keep a collaborative mindset focused on mutual purpose. For all the non-technical people reading, do your homework to empathize with the developers. Respect their work. If you fulfill your own role well, they will respect you.

15: Dominant Behavior [Career]

Pay careful attention to the subtleties in a person's behavior. This is crucial when interacting with people in more powerful, senior positions than you. This is the big boss about to offer you a job or your manager contemplating your promotion. Focus on *how* your counterparty communicates; it will showcase their personality and their perception of you. When and if you rise to a position of power, your awareness of these subtle details will come in handy.

If you're young and pursuing a career in software, I'll put two hundred bucks down that says you're feeling restless in your current position. You've grown fatigued from tinkering with the same codebase, you hear about your startup friends cashing out from fat Google acquisitions, and you've read way too many "How Much Money Do Software Developers Make?" articles on Quora. All these tiny needles keep pricking at your personal concept of developer adequacy. Aside from these distractions, there are the omnipresent success stories and the purposeful neglect of failure stories, mixed together with a huge pool of career options. It's easy to see why developers get itchy feet.

What's this got to do with dominant behavior? This restlessness translates into a continuous cycle of job seeking, where you find yourself moving from one job to another every couple of years. Consequently, this puts you back on the interview circuit more often than you would probably like. Once you're back on that circuit, you're once again faced with these kinds of one-sided, power-based situations.

In early 2014, I had been working at Qualcomm for about four years when I started to apply to startups. I was completely sucked into the startup hype, and I had read my fair share of Paul Graham essays. Paul is well-known for co-founding Y Combinator, a famous American institution that trains, grows, and mentors startups. My colleagues and I, living far away from Silicon Valley in sunny San Diego, used his blog posts to get a glimpse into the trendy world of startups. Was working at a startup as cool as everyone made it out to be? Did they really give you free food and have cold brew coffee on tap? Could they make you rich? I wanted to find out.

At Qualcomm, they instituted something known as "Matrix Management," whereby your manager and your direct supervisor were two different people. Your manager—the person responsible for your bonuses and promotions—had nothing to do with your actual day-to-day work. Your direct supervisor—your day-to-day boss—was the one who assigned your daily tasks and had little to do with your career prospects or financial gain within the company. Every six months you'd have a performance review. This started with your selection of five trustworthy colleagues who could speak truthfully, and hopefully positively, about you and your work. These peer reviews were then relayed to your manager, who

scored your overall performance in a variety of categories between 1 and 5.

The managers of entry-level developers were
mid-level employees—the majority of whom Qualcomm
has a tight chokehold over—pummeled by the day-to-
day stress of their own workloads. For them, the added
responsibility of managing was merely a bonus added to
their salary, coupled with the drudgery of sifting through
a pile of feedback twice a year.
They had little reason to care
about our career paths or personal goals. My manager sat in
a completely different building
than me, and every six months
I would have to re-remind him
of what I had been working on.
This managerial apathy certainly wasn't making me feel very
enthusiastic about my job.

> My manager sat in a
> completely different
> building than
> me, and every six
> months I would have
> to re-remind him
> of what I had been
> working on.

Another contributing factor to my career anxiety was
a general feeling of disconnect. In terms of people, imagine what it feels like to be one of thousands and thousands of developers. You are software engineer #2513.
I had a one-on-one with a director of engineering twice
during my entire time with the company: once to receive
a firm handshake off the back of a promotion, and again
after I'd handed in my notice.

As far as the work went, I never felt connected with
it; it never felt like *my* work. I had a reasonable sense

of how my code contributed to Qualcomm as a whole, but the tiny-cog-in-a-giant-machine sensation weighed heavy on me. To add to my uneasiness, two major projects I had worked on were canned after months of hard work. All of this made startups all the more attractive. I was young, had few responsibilities, and didn't mind putting my retirement plan on hold.

I began to apply and interview for startup jobs. It was amazing to see the kind of intimacy within these small companies. Everyone fit in a room. Everyone knew each other's name. I was infatuated with it all. After four years of working for a large corporation, the startup grass definitely looked greener. I would find out later, of course, that nothing is sunshine and rainbows forever.

During my tenure with a couple startups, I had two significant interactions with two different CEOs. What they said was roughly the same, but *how* they said it made all the difference. Breaking down each experience reveals important nuances between two vastly different CEOs.

In one interview, the CEO walked in, shook my hand, sat down, leaned back in his chair, and very casually put his feet up on the table. I was shocked. I had never seen anyone do anything like this in a professional setting before. At the time, I brushed it off. I was still wearing rose-tinted glasses—this was just another normal part of startup culture, and startup culture was where I wanted to be.

From the outside, it might seem like this wasn't a big deal—like it was an entrepreneur challenging the status quo, breaking the job interview boundaries, and welcoming me into the "family." But in truth it was a subtle display of power. Without anything being said, I immediately felt "in my place." I was the humble developer, eager to make a good impression, praying to land the job. This guy was clearly in his comfort zone and was dominating the room. It was obvious that he was the decision-maker for the company—*I* was coming to work for *him*.

A couple years later, I found myself in the same situation, sitting across the room from another startup CEO, being interviewed for a developer position. Only this time the CEO sat upright in his chair and faced me directly. We had a conversation that was similar to the other; he asked me questions and I answered them as best I could. But this felt different. This felt positive, equal, and respectful. This CEO gave off an air of "*Let's work together*" as opposed to the previous example's air of "*Maybe you can come work for me.*"

These subtle behaviors showcase the deep traits found behind the personalities of each and every one of us. Both of these CEOs were great leaders, but their styles were as different as night and day. The first CEO stayed hands-off. We didn't see him around the office often. He came to provide feedback at product demos and checked up on everyone at a high level. The second CEO was a boots-on-the-ground operator. He would be jumping on a sales call, explaining business concepts to us over dinner, and logged more hours in the office than any other employee. They say you should never judge a book by its cover, but in some cases, the cover might be extremely important.

I can't stress enough the significance of behavior and body language. When making a career or life-altering decision, focus hard on your interactions when you're with anyone in a position of power over you. This will happen often. Stay conscious of actions that exude aggression, dominance, or power. Your initial judgement of character may save you a lot of time.

16: Full-Stack [Learning]

For any developer, the raw amount of knowledge to gain can feel extremely overwhelming. Sometimes, when there are too many options for learning, we can become paralyzed before we even start. *Am I working on the right things? Is this the correct language to study? Is this technology even relevant anymore?* Learning is a life-long process, and the horizon of knowledge stretches further into the distance as we progress.

This chapter focuses on a common question, *how much do I need to know*? People just dipping their toes into technology will often ponder this question. *Do I have to be good at math to code? How much do I need to know about computer science? What about hardware or software? What is it that software developers learn, as opposed to a CS major?* All these questions and many more might be running around in your head. My answer to them all is that you don't have to learn everything—which is unreasonable—but you need to be aware of everything on a basic level.

> Learning is a life-long process, and the horizon of knowledge stretches further into the distance as we progress.

In the world of computers, there are many layers. Imagine a huge stack of technology. At the bottom of the stack we have electrons, science, and raw physics. At the top of the stack we have code, web browsers, and fancy IDEs. Wedged between the two we have a *ton* of stuff. How much of this stack do we have to understand to get ahead?

> *"You don't have to know the details about each layer, but you should be able to talk about each one on a basic level."*

> *– Bruce H. Krogh*

Professor Krogh had a profound impact on me as a student. He taught a wide variety of introductory courses at CMU. I had him for Analog Circuits, Signals and Systems, and Introduction to Computer Engineering. These are all vastly different subjects and he was teaching all of them at university level. Professor Krogh enjoyed randomly calling on students during lectures with random questions that sometimes went off on huge tangents. I got the impression that he just enjoyed seeing his students squirm. He once asked me for five examples of how companies use GPS. I managed three examples and blanked out right before he moved on to the next unlucky student.

Regardless of what class he was teaching, he would always repeat that quote during the first week. He consistently preached the value of a solid foundation and I credit him as the reason I do likewise. He had one particular slide that he would often refer to—a picture of the all-powerful stack of computing. For everything we learned, he would show us that image and indicate where our new knowledge fit into the grand scheme of things. I was in awe of his understanding of technology, as well as his ability to take disparate parts of computing and distill them down into shared concepts. I always thought to myself, *how can one guy know so much?*

Let's go back to our mental model of the stack. On the very bottom we have electricity, at the very top we have code, and we have a lot of stuff in between. When you break down one layer of the stack, there will be more and more layers to break down; it never ends. Let's take a quick walk through this stack together.

First, let's separate hardware from software—that's two easy layers. We'll put hardware on the bottom and software on the top. Let's break down hardware first. We'll split it up into three basic levels: circuit design, CPU design, and HW system architecture.

A circuit designer is someone who meticulously designs a specific circuit that performs a specific function. For example, let's say they're designing a high-performance arithmetic logic unit (ALU) that can add, subtract, multiply, and divide ones and zeros efficiently. They're making sure this ALU is the best ALU in the world. That's their job, and they do it extremely well.

On the next level above, we have a CPU designer who is in charge of creating an entire processor. They need an ALU—maybe a few of them—that will fit into the processor. Along with that, they need a variety of other hardware components to make sure the CPU is up to spec and performant. The CPU designer will utilize the work of a diverse set of circuit designers to put together his or her masterpiece.

On top of the CPU designer is the HW system architect. The architect will be in charge of designing a holistic computing system. They need a multitude of different processors and modules. Let's assume they're working on a next-generation smartphone. It needs a powerful quad-core apps processor to run the latest-and-greatest Android operating system. It needs a state-of-the-art GPU to let users play immersive video games. Don't forget the modem, which will enable the phone to connect to local base stations and make calls. To top it off, the HW Architect wants some kind of motion processor so the phone can detect twists, turns, and your daily steps. Besides the demanding list of unique processing units, the system also needs memories and caches to run efficiently. All these different processors and hardware modules will come together and create a system that will eventually live inside this new cell phone.

We just broke hardware down into three very generic layers. You could take each one of those layers and break it down even further—it would never end. Let's switch gears to software now. We'll do the same thing and split software into three generic layers: Firmware, OS Level, and Application Development.

A firmware, or embedded, developer will be working on low-level code. This might be the code that executes before an operating system is even loaded. This is code that runs with very limited resources and may have no concept of dynamic memory allocation. If you have a PC, this is that black BIOS "boot-up" screen that pops open right after you hit the power button. For any hardware to be useful, there must be some software running on it; if we didn't have software, all our cool hardware would be equivalent to bricks. Embedded developers build the software that sits directly on top of the hardware. They provide essential interfaces to higher level software, allowing it to take control of the hardware itself.

Go up one level and you step into the world of OS developers. These are the guru Linux Kernel developers who push the boundaries of how efficiently software can be run. They'll handle process scheduling, file system management, and security. How can hundreds of processes run side-by-side on a computer without the whole thing crashing? How can the buggy code you write not bring down the entire system? That's OS magic for you. If you have a simplistic system like a microwave, perhaps an operating system is unnecessary. But for any intelligent computing device, it's essential.

Finally, let's look at application development. Most of us developers work on this layer. This is where all the games are made, where millions of apps are developed, where the shiny web portals get built. We're at the top of the stack now and it's a very, very busy place. The demand for application development is high and will forever stay high.

So, what does it mean to be a full-stack developer? Web development is hyped up these days. It's what ninety-nine percent of startup tech is all about, it's what nearly every single business needs, and it's why the Internet is the Internet. Web development is an extremely high-leverage software field to be in and for good reason. No one goes to the store and buys plastic boxes with installation CDs anymore—everything you'd ever need is a click away in your Chrome browser.

Remember, web development is a very small part of application development and application development is a very small part of the software stack. Remember also that our software stack owes its very existence to the colossal hardware stack below it. Web development is a very, very tiny sliver in the mighty stack of computing.

This is why I think the term full-stack is misleading and borderline deceptive. In modern lingo, this term is only ever used in the context of web programming. Within web development, full-stack means two things: you can write some front-end code that runs in a browser, and you can write some server-side code that runs on a computer somewhere. However, if you went up to a Linux Systems programmer and asked him or her if they were full-stack, they would smack you in the face. The modern definition of full-stack simply means you can write web applications, nothing more.

When I think of full-stack, I think of the full-stack of computing. This is hardware that carries the electrons through its metal and all the software that turns it off and on. This is the stack that we should all strive to understand and appreciate. The concept of full-stack should create feelings of awe in everyone by showcasing how incredible computing really is. This is the real foundation. I cringe when I hear people calling themselves full-stack developers when all they know about is one web framework and some JavaScript.

Being pedantic about titles is not what's important. What is important is our basic understanding of these essential technical building blocks. Everything you learn—from low-level digital circuit design all the way up to high-level web development—has a position in the full-stack of computing. We don't need to be an expert in everything, but we must understand each piece on a basic level.

17: Non-Technical Trying To Be Technical [Stories]

Patrick, mechanical engineer turned coder, is back with a whirlwind story about his first job as a developer. Peeking under the covers of professional software development, this story shows just how messy the reality can be. Patrick's CMU training helps him survive in tough development environments, but you'll see how this pressure-cooker experience is hard on many.

My first foray into mobile development was as an iOS developer for a newspaper publisher. Aside from a few stories, I was unfamiliar with professional software development and I was relatively new to mobile as a platform. I majored in mechanical engineering but was drawn to coding soon after graduation. Back then I was a complete beginner.

Somehow, a big fancy media company wanted to hire me to build their flagship mobile product. Opportunity was knocking. I took them up on their offer and started prepping for my first professional job as a mobile developer. I was employed alongside others to build native apps, on all platforms, for all devices. My job was to work on the iPad version of their newspaper app.

Even though I had no real understanding of what "doing it the right way" meant, I'm pretty sure that the company I worked for was doing it the wrong way. All due credit, though—here were media professionals stepping out of their comfort zone and building a technical product from scratch with no prior experience. Imagine your super-niche engineering research center creating a beautifully crafted newspaper filled with well-researched articles—much easier said than done.

> *Even though I had no real understanding of what "doing it the right way" meant, I'm pretty sure that the company I worked for was doing it the wrong way.*

Everything starts with the hiring. Intuitively, they did the right thing—they hired senior staff first. Where might a media company go to source senior technologists? Their strategy was to jump on Amazon.com, search for the highest-rated technical books, and contact the authors. If you wrote a book about Apple's iOS, you must be pretty good, right?

These were the early days of mobile development, when Apple's documentation was somewhat lackluster. Developers writing about iOS frameworks were rare. Anyone who had any experience using these arcane libraries appeared invaluable.

For anyone who's never developed on iOS before, they have a client-side persistence library called CoreData. In a nutshell, this is the ORM—object-relational mapping—for iOS. An ORM is an invaluable aid for any developer modeling out business logic. These libraries enable you to set up complex relationships between objects, allow for intuitive querying of information, and provide basic scaffolding to make sure your data persists properly. My company had found *the* CoreData guy through Amazon. He had written the highest-rated CoreData book, so he must have been one of the best. What could go possibly go wrong?

The publishers offered him an absurd amount of money to head up their new iOS team. I give this guy a lot of props—this is a prime example of a developer taking advantage of the trends. Unfortunately, knowing an iOS library inside out does not mean you have the skills to head up and run an entire engineering department.

With the senior staff installed, they moved to fill out the engineering department. The back-end had been contracted out, so they were looking to hire programmers purely for their Apple/iOS expertise. You don't need that many people to develop a client-side application—two to four reasonably skilled developers can get the job done. Any more and there are way too many cooks in the kitchen. I believe we hired about thirty engineers to work on one single iOS application! The company's mindset was, *the more money we throw at this, the better it will be*, and they had a *lot* of money. The hiring process was insane, but I'm not one to complain—they hired me, after all.

One day on the job, I got an email from an excited hiring manager saying she had just hired a new iOS developer. This developer was supposedly really talented and had even shown up to the interview with an impressive demo on his phone. In those days, not many people showed up to interviews with live portfolios, so naturally, I was also pretty excited. The hiring manager had taped the demo and was hyping it up—there were awesome graphics, cool physics, and some interactive gameplay. I checked out the footage and instantly recognized the app—I had built the same one! It was a template app from a popular online tutorial. The app showed a bunch of bouncing balls that you could interact with. There was nothing ground-breaking about it, just a stock physics engine, some fancy assets, and plug-and-play gesture recognizers.

These terms may sound fancy, but these features come straight out of the box these days—kind of like a steering wheel on a car. A physics engine can determine how a ball bounces with gravity, how two soccer players collide, or how water overflows out of a teapot. Gesture recognizers give you precise feedback signals when you pinch, drag, or swipe on the screen. In modern software, it's just a matter of gluing things together—no one re-invents the wheel. Obviously, our non-technical hiring managers hadn't known any better.

And this is how they filled out the engineering team. There was a deadline, a ton of money to be burned, and programmers to hire. This developer, who had been coding for less than six months, was able to land a full-time job—with a decent salary—off the back of a demo app from the Internet! When he showed up for work, it was immediately apparent that he had no idea what he was doing. Somehow, he floated around for the duration of the project; no one was ever quite sure what he was up to.

The project management was appalling. There were no code reviews of any kind. There was no development process. There were no branching or merging patterns with source control. Everything came down to raw Git commits, poorly resolved coding conflicts, and a lot of crashes in production. A few senior engineers tried their best to maintain sanity, but junior engineers were busy pumping out untested code while a set of floaters wandered around like headless chickens. Periodically,

people would come by my
desk and ask me—the 23-year-
old entry-level developer—if
there was anything they could
work on.

> *Wherever you end up, train yourself to function independently, no matter how chaotic it may be.*

After a year and a lot of
Objective-C code, I began to
really appreciate my CMU train-
ing. All those obscure coding labs and open-ended projects classes made this job seem like a cake-walk. I was
already accustomed to digging my way out of darkness
to reach lofty ten-thousand-foot-high goals. However,
this unstructured environment paralyzed many of my
colleagues. Hand-holding curriculums and online tutorials had not prepared them for this. For anyone transitioning from academia to industry, do not underestimate how drastically different the environment can be;
you might unknowingly be stepping into a zoo of code.
There's nothing you can do about the environment, but
there's always something you can do about your reac-
tion. Wherever you end up, train yourself to function independently, no matter how chaotic it may be.

Despite the insanity, the company eventually managed to ship product. Somehow, thirty engineers committing directly to the Master Branch still managed to
create something that was seen by millions of people.
Unfortunately, our apps eventually flopped and are now
resting in peace in the app graveyard.

18: Respect Every Position [Daily Life]

My friend Tammy is back. After re-inventing herself post-graduation, she found an amazing group of people at a food startup. Unfortunately, startups go through some bad apples. One of the bigger apples was Tammy's ex-CTO. A common characteristic of developers is to undervalue the importance of other departments. Too often, I've seen egotistical programmers who think their code runs the show. These are dangerous sentiments and can kill any working environment.

Earlier in my career, I worked under an unpleasant CTO who gained a reputation for making our employees cry. I was working at an early startup that had recently promoted an engineer with the emotional intelligence of a brick into the highest ranking technical position in the company. What ensued was tough to stomach. I don't have any positive memories about that individual, but his actions highlight the countless ways a developer should *not* act.

During my first couple of months on the job, one of my colleagues from customer service brought a fresh customer complaint to our CTO. It was a startup, so funds were limited and everyone shared the same space in an open plan office. This meant zero privacy—all conversations were public. The first time the service rep came by with the complaint, she was met with a curt, abrupt response from the CTO:

"They're not using the site properly. Link them to the documentation."

This is a classic engineering response to any problem. Unfortunately, it's not very helpful for someone dealing with a customer. The interaction didn't sit well with me. *Is this guy really brushing this off that easily?*

Fast-forward a couple days, and the same rep kept coming back with more complaints from different customers about the same issue. Obviously, there was a problem. To my surprise, our CTO was still not giving her the time of day! I was starting to get frustrated, but I was two months into the job and not ready to tell our chief technologist how to behave. Finally, the fourth time around, he decided to take a closer look at the issue. Turned out the customer was using our website correctly; unsurprisingly, there was a bug in the code. Why wasn't that his first instinct?

It was this interaction, and many more that followed, that convinced me this guy was a jerk. First, his lack of respect for the customer service representative was crystal clear. She was doing her job and didn't need to be subjected to such demeaning, negative behavior. By the third time she had approached him about the problem, she'd started to tear up from the stress. Second, it showed a blatantly arrogant thought-process. A software bug was the *last* possibility. The most likely possibility in his mind was that the customer was not using the application properly. That ordering should have been reversed.

This CTO had been programming since he was practically in the womb; he got his first paying job at age 13. For over half his life, he had been getting paid to write code. Technically, I'm sure he was the best of the best. Unfortunately, being a prodigy coder doesn't translate into becoming an effective leader. He was socially awkward and held on tight to an entitled persona of *"I'm worth a lot"*—a too-common trait among developers.

> *At a small startup, every single person's job is crucial.*

Our CTO had a toxic complex in which he believed that his position was more important than anyone else's. This is where he went horribly wrong. At a small startup, every single person's job is crucial. If the customer service representative stops answering phone calls, the company will fail. If the accountant stops sending out invoices, the company will fail. If the CEO stops traveling, people don't get paid. As software developers, we must never think of ourselves as above any other roles or departments. The mentality should never be *"I,"* it should always be *"only possible together."*

The above was an example of disrespect towards fellow employees, but our CTO also had a severe lack of respect for the company as a whole. During his brief tenure, he was working on a book about Redis. Redis is a popular open-source software that many people use to store data and speed up their applications. What's important to note here is that Redis had absolutely nothing to do with our company. It's a software tool we utilized, but it was not related whatsoever to the business, our product, or the company mission. It was purely a hobby, a side project for our CTO. But he used our system as a guinea pig to test out strange Redis experiments to include in his book!

This act was negatively disruptive to the company. By using the company's projects as a testbed for Redis, he created insurmountable obscurity and unnecessary complexity for the team. No one else had any idea how our caching worked. This chokepoint slowed development down to a crawl. This behavior goes against all reasonable software development practice. When working with a team, it should be a priority to disseminate knowledge, increase transparency, enable developers to jump into different parts of the system, and avoid single points of failure. Doing experiments for a personal book does not fall into any of those categories.

We are human, and no one—on any level—is immune to dangerous personality habits.

Even though the CTO was a technical guru, he was an ill-fit for the role. In my career, I have seen countless engineers hold a similar, and similarly dangerous, sense of entitlement that ruins company cultures. This ranges from the developer who thinks he or she writes the best code, to the VP of Engineering who dictates how other departments inter-act with developers. We are human, and no one—on any level—is immune to dangerous personality habits.

19: The Blessing Of Grunt Work [Learning]

Grunt work is a blessing in disguise. For any level of development, there is a huge pile of mundane, inane, no-one-wants-to-do-it work. It will be dumped on top of you at some point in your career, most often when you're the newest, most junior member of the team. This could be anything from six hours of pixel-pushing to a month's worth of technical debt refactoring. It's like picking up a bunch of rocks just so you can put them down someplace else. As an entry-level developer, you'll be given an early dose of grunt work in some companies simply as a way of vetting you. This usually reduces to a slow sprinkle once you've proven your skills. Do not be discouraged; each of these mundane tasks is an invaluable seed for learning.

As an entry-level developer, you'll be given an early dose of grunt work in some companies simply as a way of vetting you.

My first software internship was in the beautiful state of Colorado. I was responsible for porting installers across operating system platforms—one of the most prestigious tasks in any software company. For those too young to know about installers, there was a time long ago when you actually had to travel to a store in the real world to buy software. This is how software was once distributed—we didn't always have the all-powerful cloud.

First, let's get a frame of reference for installers. Think of installers as huge, complex, software state machines. *What happens if they cancel the install at this step? Did we set up all the directory and file permissions properly? What if an older version is already installed? How do we update the registry? How do we clean up the registry? What if the disk is full mid-install? How do you uninstall?*

Could we have a moment's silence for developers everywhere? I was in fifth grade when I started playing Diablo. When I first installed the game, I couldn't fathom what software was. I didn't realize that there were developers—real life human beings—out there somewhere writing code so I could kill demons and drink mana potions. I certainly didn't think about the fact that there were developers out there who wrote Diablo's installer! I didn't give it a second's thought; I just watched the bar crawl all the way to one hundred percent with baited breath. But now here I was, a developer writing installer code. For every interface you touch, every button you see, and all the plumbing you don't see, there are coders out there making sure it all works.

Initially, I was pretty bummed when presented with this project. It sounded excruciatingly boring. I thought I was in for an unproductive internship. Was I really going to put installer porting on my résumé? I wanted to work on *real* software. The company had already ported its application code over to Linux and all that was left to do was to package it all up. Unglamorous as it sounds, this project turned out to be one of my most rewarding experiences.

I gained invaluable knowledge that summer. Those three months developing installers laid the foundations for many of the skills that I use today. As a prerequisite for the project, I was forced to learn the ins and outs of Linux. I get nostalgic thinking about those days. I had to read about basic file permissions, learn about the obscurely named top-level directories, and struggle with configurations to get my source code to compile. That summer in Colorado was instrumental in my career.

The coding was a next-level exercise in attention to detail. Unless you've developed a ridiculously complicated state machine, not many people appreciate the many nuances and complexities of an install process. You have to update the registries properly. You need to set up the proper permissions across all the new files. You need to make sure all temporary directories are cleaned up. You need to ensure the software uninstalls and upgrades properly. Everything has to be triple-verified. It was a level of detail that I had never experienced before. If the software fails to install or update, you may as well tell the end user they should use somebody else's app, because yours is broken. The devil is always in the details, and the details make us better developers.

Years later, history would repeat itself when I went through a similar situation as a full-time developer. I expected to get my first load of grunt work early and it came through the door on day one. My first assignment was to revamp an old MAKE system and move it over to a then-shiny new Python software-building solution called

In software development, you'll get one fun task for every ten mind-numbing ones.

Scons. If you have ever had the pleasure of using MAKE outside of homework, I'm sure you know that this task was no joke. That project single-handedly forced me to understand software building on a very deep level. It was another technical level-up for me and my career.

In software development, you'll get one fun task for every ten mind-numbing ones. If you're working at a super small shop, you might be lucky enough to have only green pastures ahead of you, where you can cowboy around all day long. But for anyone working in a larger setting, there will be no shortage of mundane work waiting for you. You might be porting build systems or sifting through code that was written eight years ago. I urge you to take on these tasks eagerly. Don't underestimate this kind of work—it might build the foundation for lifelong skills.

20: Lessons Learned [Career]

During my time at Qualcomm, I was part of a tight-knit, fresh-out-of-college group of engineers. We had been hired in new-graduate batches and quickly formed the kind of camaraderie that comes with the circumstance. After a few years of developing chipsets and getting used to Qualcomm's product cycle, many of us started turning our heads in the direction of startups—the grass looked greener over in Silicon Valley. My friend Daniel was the first one of our group to take a leap of faith. He was leaving us, his fat stocks, that nice 401k, and all our comfy Qualcomm benefits to test the startup waters. Many of us, myself included, would follow in his footsteps. This is a small sample of Dan's journey and is packed with valuable insights.

> *Managing a developer is very different than managing a codebase.*

Shortly after transitioning into the startup world, I became a technical lead for the first time. As I fumbled my way through managerial responsibilities, I went through an amazing period of personal growth. Managing a developer is very different than managing a codebase. This first managerial experience was ultimately a failure in the practical sense, but it provided me with many useful lessons. This all took place at a tiny fitness startup in Los Angeles.

Hiring Without Desperation

We were desperate. Our engineering team, once numbering a healthy five developers, had dwindled down to two people. Like many other tiny startups, we were little kids fighting for Venture Capitalist attention with a laundry list of ambitious and poorly prioritized technical goals—goals that were now impossibilities. We weren't making any money, and the future of the company hung on our CEO's salesmanship and the sexiness of our next demo. Actually, *desperate* was an understatement.

Debt has both technical and cultural forms, both of which can crush you.

I ran through the gamut of difficult emotions during that time—anxiety, sadness, fear, doubt. Making any kind of decision while maintaining a calm and balanced state of mind is much easier said than done. We didn't want our startup to die, and two engineers simply weren't going to cut it. Product needed to be built and we needed someone to build it—anyone.

The first mistake I made was to hire too fast. At the time, I hadn't fathomed the magnitude of my responsibility. The only thing on my mind was getting someone in the door who could code. I wasn't too concerned about who that someone was. There are a million things going against you when you're hiring for a startup. You're strapped for cash, you can't meet candidate expectations for salaries, and you have an uphill battle to face when selling the mission. Furthermore, the time spent recruiting takes you away from the four hundred other urgent things you need to be working on. Nevertheless, the recruiting needed to get done.

My core blunder was to prioritize speed over the long-term well-being of the company. If you're feeling rushed by recruitment pressure, take a step back and slow, down. Hiring must be done with extreme care. If you don't find the right candidate—even when the company is desperate—it means you have to keep looking. I saved a little bit of time up front, only to be overwhelmed later. Debt has both technical and cultural forms, both of which can crush you.

The second mistake I made was that I didn't interview hard enough. I didn't ask challenging questions, I didn't dig, and I didn't uncover the candidate's true technical abilities until it was too late. I had nice-guy syndrome. During each interview, I was reserved and reluctant. I gave people the benefit of the doubt and utterly failed at my primary objective: to technically vet each candidate. After a few hours of easy questions and reasonably pleasant conversations, I rationalized that they should be good enough and we sent over offers.

Here is the lesson—do not give any technical benefit of the doubt to your candidates. You may be thinking: *this candidate is probably having a bad day, perhaps I'm asking the wrong questions, or maybe they don't interview well.* While it's perfectly normal for a candidate to have a bad day—I've bombed plenty of interviews—it doesn't mean you shouldn't dig as the interviewer. If you're positive they're technically competent, start getting to know them as a person. If they are technically incompetent, stop the interview and thank them for their time. If you didn't get enough info, schedule an additional meeting to get the reassurance you need.

We were desperate for an engineer and we got one. Let's call him Joe. Hiring Joe was a precursor to many months of stress and many more lessons learned.

No Scapegoating

It wasn't long before I realized that hiring Joe was a huge mistake. I then began aiming all my negative emotions at Joe. The product was late because Joe wasn't a strong developer. The technical debt was piling up because Joe couldn't get familiar with the system. Having never been a manager before, it was convenient and natural for me to have these feelings. I guarantee that all of us have directed blame—even if it's just in our heads—at our colleagues at some point. Eventually, I realized that Joe was *completely* my responsibility as his manager. No reasonable leader, under any amount of technical stress, should ever make a scapegoat of one of their team members.

With that said, let's not tiptoe around the fact that Joe was a novice. Joe's level of experience made him a dangerous developer. He was obviously a beginner, but he had coded enough to not need hand-holding. To be honest, I would have preferred Joe know *less* so I could have guided him more. Joe knew enough to run on his own, enough to push out commits. Unfortunately, these commits did more harm than good to our codebase. Joe couldn't sense how his changes affected the system holistically, he didn't check for edge cases, and his code would often melt down our existing features.

As Joe kept pushing out spaghetti code, I became increasingly bitter about the state of affairs. When our CEO complained to me about the latest malfunctions in the demo, I mentally abused Joe. Among peers, blame can be divvied up—no harm, no foul. However, on a team, the blame must always fall on the shoulders of the leader. If you accept the role, you accept the responsibility.

As a leader, you should never direct blame at your developers. When these feelings arise, always reflect on *your* core responsibilities. I eventually realized that I had neglected my duties to train and onboard my team. While some coders may come up to speed quickly, others will be slow and will make more errors. This is not *their* fault or *their* problem. I needed to take extra time and sit with Joe to make him an effective member of the team. Any blaming or complaining must be replaced by constructive actions.

Maintaining Clear Expectations & Goals

I failed to set clear expectations with Joe. I expected a lot from him, but unfortunately these thoughts only existed in my head. Without communicated expectations, you have nothing. While it's normal for expectations to be a dynamic rollercoaster, it's dangerous to have them be opaque—or even worse, nonexistent. In the best-case scenario, you should cover every expectation you have for your team and their work, from basic coding standards all the way up to career progression. *Should we document our code? Is it cool to add in these libraries? When do we qualify something as done? What's the big picture of my contribution over the next couple of years? What do you expect out of me as an employee?* The answers to these questions must be clear and upfront.

Being close to our CEO at the time, I was in tune with our company's goals, even as they fluctuated over time. Unfortunately, I took this for granted. In the beginning, Joe and I spoke very briefly about near-term objectives and our development process. I was anxious for Joe to jump into the code. I assumed he was a fortuneteller who would magically keep on my wavelength.

Keeping a group of professionals aligned over a period of time is no easy feat. Imagine a place where everyone knows what they're working on, why they're working on it, and how it fits into the big picture. Think that's hard? Try keeping that going over a few years.

This kind of synergy is not the result of a simple new-hire meeting or onboarding document. It comes from clear expectations, consistent communication, and perpetual realignments. In a software company, the only constant is change. As we chugged along, I assumed Joe's automatic alignment without verbalizing any expectations. If the CEO changed direction or asked us to scrap a feature, I *assumed* Joe would simply understand. When expectations aren't clear and people don't understand the *why* behind their tasks, quality work is impossible.

I had never set goals for Joe, and therefore I was never able to quantify his performance. I was naïve. I wanted him to learn new languages, pick up our frameworks, get pumped up on the mission, and follow all our design patterns. And I wanted him to do this all automatically, without a word from me. How could anyone understand all of that without clear, explicit leadership?

Expectations play a crucial role in any kind of relationship. If you think a team member needs to spend two months getting better at C++, then tell them so and make it a written goal. If you expect a team member to document their work, make sure you consider the feature complete only when you see a polished Wiki entry. Expectations will always change over the lifetime of the relationship, but you should always be clear about them—never assume anything.

Constant Communication

Setting clear expectations is a lofty and abstract goal. It is implemented concretely via constant communication. I had always imagined a startup as a magical place. I had pictured a big LAN party where you could shoot the breeze, eat pizza, and rid yourself of petty bureaucracy—wasn't that the dream? Everyone would vibe with each other, there wouldn't need to be any meetings, and you could crank on code and drink Mountain Dew all day. While this might make for an interesting movie scene, it's not what any successful company looks like—no matter the size.

During college, I loved the hacker way of doing things. I secretly enjoyed the marathon coding sessions, having a huge bag of chips next to my keyboard, and splitting a pizza with my friends. When I landed my first job, the politics and environment were a reality check. It felt mind-numbing compared to school; everything was slow, political, and it didn't feel fun anymore. It was this that made startups seem so alluring. To me, startups were a way to relive the glory days of late-night coding.

Armed with an agenda and a purpose, a thirty-minute meeting turns into a highly productive exchange.

Obviously, the hacker mindset does not translate into effective leadership. I had always scoffed at one-on-ones with my managers. They were grossly unproductive for me during my first corporate job, so I felt no reason to conduct them with Joe.

Speaking as someone who used to dread meetings, I cannot stress enough how important they are. Since this experience, I have put in immeasurable time preparing and conducting effective meetings. The people who underestimate meetings are the ones who do not know how to utilize them. Armed with an agenda and a purpose, a thirty-minute meeting turns into a highly productive exchange. Furthermore, the one-on-one meeting is the cornerstone of management. It is where thoughts are shared, expectations aligned, and assumptions laid to rest. For anyone dipping their toes into management, take the time to read about how to conduct one-on-ones—any kind of management is doomed without them.

Vulnerability is OK

During this mismanagement ordeal, it took me far too long to bring it up with my CEO. The root cause was my personal fear of being seen as incapable; I didn't want to be that guy who couldn't handle the situation. I was the one who had hired Joe. I kept telling myself that I could make it work. That thought stemmed from a mix of fear and ego. What I learned is that it's completely unreasonable to take the full weight of a difficult situation onto your shoulders. There will be times when you will need to ask for help, and somebody will gladly give it. When they look back to you, you'll return the favor.

Conclusion

This is a common storyline for many first-time technical leads. If you go through a variation of this, stay attentive and conscious of the situation. Even a seemingly simple assignment of mentoring one person should be considered a serious endeavor.

My failure was bucketed into two categories. The first was my mindset. I never took responsibility as the lead. Joe was my scapegoat, the reason for our failed demos, and the cause of our spaghetti code. These issues were all things that I was accountable for. Replace blame with constructive action.

The second failure was communication. Joe and I were never clear regarding expectations. Don't assume you can operate a company like a hack-week project. Put in extra effort to organize meetings and quickly share changes that affect other people's work, and never assume your colleague "just gets it."

21: Diva Developers [Daily Life]

When my product manager (PM) friend Jane told me about "diva developers," I almost laughed out loud at the idea. Unfortunately, this wasn't a joke. A single, unrestrained developer can disrupt the flow of entire teams. Jane's story is a common one for many PMs.

A previous ecommerce company I work for created an unfortunate and unforgivable slang term to describe a certain type of developer. I've heard a lot of nonsense titles—rock stars, 10x coders, wizards—but never anything as sad as a "diva developer." When I first heard the phrase in conversation, I wanted to believe it was a joke. Slowly but surely, though, I accepted my new Silicon Valley reality. There were some very entitled programmers who fit the term perfectly. These are programmers with a little extra ego, a little less empathy, who constantly put themselves at the center of any situation—they don't move with the team; the team has to rotate around them. Their behavior is so bold and entitled that it negatively affects everyone they work with.

> *At a software company, the ultimate gatekeepers of progress are the developers. Sometimes the only thing we can do is play nice with them.*

As a PM, I work with many different departments—design, engineering, strategy, analytics, marketing—and I do my best to get along with everyone. That's part and parcel of the job. Yet regardless of how benevolent I think I am or how much others like working with me, my main concern boils down to one thing—progress. Progress is what product managers stress about. It's what we complain to our friends about and it's what keeps us up at night. Worst of all, it's also the one thing we have minimal control over. At a software company, the ultimate gatekeepers of progress are the developers. Sometimes the only thing we can do is play nice with them.

On one of my first projects, I had to coordinate with a remote team of developers in China. Despite the logistical hurdles of limited real-time communication, time zone differentials, and the language barrier, we worked well together. Requirements were clearly communicated, development moved at a consistent pace, and there was a strong bond across the team.

Our mojo took a hit when our first local developer joined the team. Despite having a good thing going between our remote offices, the company was putting in an effort to co-locate its developers. I was scared of having our development split across the world, but I tried my best to count the potential blessings. Now I could actually speak with someone face to face and get more in the know with the daily tech. Little did I realize that this new developer was a diva and would soon be wreaking havoc on our dynamic.

Our new local developer, Martin, was obsessed with code quality. An extra pair of eyes on the codebase quickly turned into a constant bashing of our software; every remark out of Martin's mouth was a barbed stab about how awful the existing implementations were. Instead of being constructive and striving to be part of the collective, Martin distanced himself from the other coders with continuous harsh, accusatory comments. A few weeks in, I was stressing out.

Regarding managerial duties, our remote developers were sitting alongside their technical leads and managers in China. Their development flow was humming smoothly, and they only communicated with me for product issues. We also had a local engineering department, but their attention at the time was focused on different product lines.

This proved to be tricky for our team, because Martin was assigned a local manager who was unfamiliar with our product and our style of development. His priorities were getting Martin up to speed and helping the company get engineers under one roof. Unfortunately, and understandably, this turned into Martin's supervisor only looking out for him, while not fully considering his Chinese teammates across the world. During initiation, Martin's boss informed me that Martin would be spending his first months onboarding and learning the system.

As his very first project, Martin decided to rewrite a huge feature of our application—shopping cart and checkout. The implementation was old, but it was working. I agree that it could have used some improvements, but I didn't think it warranted an overhaul—if it ain't broke, don't fix it. There was a large amount of state and validation managed by the back-end, which slowed things down for shoppers. Sure—in a perfect world, more of the state could have been managed by the browser front-end, which would only submit orders to our back-end if they were truly valid. Still, this was nowhere close to being an offensive experience for the customer. Yet Martin decided that he would take it upon himself—without telling his team—to rewrite the whole thing in JavaScript.

Unfortunately, none of us had any idea what Martin was working on until he was almost done. During his first couple of months, I assumed he was ramping up, fixing bugs, and working on standard get-up-to-speed tasks. No one expected him to rewrite one of the most important features in our product. No one had asked him to. Six weeks later, all hell broke loose when Martin was ready to push his code into production.

Right off the bat, our teammates in China were not happy. Martin had never shared anything with anyone about what he was doing. Suddenly, his teammates overseas found that he'd rewritten a huge part of the code behind their backs. They weren't upset at the new code itself; they were upset that such a huge endeavor had been initiated without their knowledge. What good is a team of coders if the developers just work in silos? For me, I was borderline raging. Almost two months of development time had passed, and we hadn't achieved anything. We'd made zero progress with larger initiatives, and the shopping cart feature looked exactly the same as it had before Martin joined. Worst of all, I now had to deal with a group of understandably disgruntled developers.

No one could discount Martin's technical skills; he had coding chops, stayed up to date with the trends, and was a natural with edge cases. Diva developers are usually good programmers, but they're completely incapable of working cooperatively as part of a team. Martin's arrogance drove him to believe that he and he alone should take on this project, without letting one single other person know about what he was doing. Not sharing his work with the team shows a total lack of respect for his colleagues, for their abilities, for the project, for its deadlines, and for the company itself. It demonstrated that he had a selfish reliance only on himself.

The ability to work as part of the collective, to be a team player, will always trump technical skill when it goes rogue.

In your journey, you will encounter many developers like this. The ability to work as part of the collective, to be a team player, will *always* trump technical skill when it goes rogue. Many 10x developers are let go due to this kind of behavior.

This story shines a light on another issue that happens often in software development: preferential treatment.

Protection from bosses and biases in favor of developers is rampant in the tech industry. Companies put developers on a pedestal. After the ordeal with Martin settled down, I felt obligated to share my thoughts with my boss and also, more importantly, with Martin's boss.

Regarding Martin's boss, I agreed with his high-level priorities—Martin was to be spending his time getting up to speed with our code. However, I crossed my fingers, hoping that he would acknowledge how Martin's behavior was disruptive to our preexisting team dynamic. Perhaps he could steer Martin in a better direction next time.

Unfortunately, that's not what happened. With minimal thought about our remote team in China, Martin's manager reassured me that this initiative was an innocent "learning project." According to him, Martin should be able to take as much time as he needed to learn the ropes and make independent decisions on how to improve the technology. In addition, Martin's reworking of the system would move more expertise to our main headquarters, something the company originally wanted.

Though I agreed that this sentiment was technically pragmatic, I still didn't think it justified secretly rewriting big features or making a whole team upset. From my perspective, Martin and his boss had simply prioritized local engineering above all else. They had little empathy for the complications added to product development, for our offended developers in China, or for the serious butterfly effect that radiated out from his actions.

Nothing came of the situation. Martin continued being Martin, and eventually the teams were reorganized, with no effort spent on remedying the situation. This obscene bias towards engineering was shocking and demoralizing to the point where I came to accept it as company culture. No one should be put up on a pedestal. Developers are valuable assets, but that doesn't mean they get a free pass to do whatever they want. Empathize with both non-technical and technical colleagues. Take time to understand what matters to other people and how your actions might adversely affect them. You might be the diva on your team, changing the entire dynamic without knowing it.

22: Leverage [Daily Life]

The word *leverage* is casually tossed around in software development and can take on different meanings across different contexts. The idea is simple, yet subtly abstract—we must focus on high-leverage activities to become effective software developers.

A high-leverage task benefits something bigger than itself and does so for an extended period of time. It is implicitly associated with a high return on investment. For example, a week spent implementing a smarter way to aggregate logs will save hours of debugging in the future. There are two parts to this definition. First, high-leverage work has the ability to elevate the work of the people around you—their jobs get easier, they gain efficiency, and the quality of their work rises. Second, high-leverage

> *A high-leverage task benefits something bigger than itself and does so for an extended period of time.*

work creates long-lasting benefits; a one-and-done type of job just doesn't cut it. Keep these two points top of mind, and work them into your daily developer habits.

Onboarding

A thorough and well-designed onboarding is a no-brainer high-leverage task. This is paramount for any organization and will dictate how efficiently developers are integrated into the flow. Thought and effort must be spent here; a good onboarding system should grow and last the lifetime of the company. There's a reason companies fly employees across the country to attend orientations.

Technical onboarding revolves heavily around your initial projects. For the engineering managers out there, take the time to think of assignments that will bring new-hire team members up to speed as effectively as possible. Consider who they have to interact with, what code they have to touch, and the progression of difficulty. For all the new developers being assimilated into established teams, put in the extra mile to integrate yourself; you'll have to do more than just that simple starter project.

Documentation

Documentation is invaluable. If possible, document your work from project inception all the way to launch. Anything from an informal technical proposal to a polished wiki page holds value. Documentation reinforces design decisions, keeps you organized, and is an excellent evergreen resource for the rest of the team. Knowledge must be persisted and disseminated. I guarantee that you will forget your own code decisions and thought processes less than a year after you made them.

Data Accessibility

It's highly likely that you will be collecting and managing data at work. Whatever it might be, your employer has deemed specific data to be precious, or else you wouldn't be collecting all those bytes. Data is an important asset. Many of your colleagues—across many departments—need access to it.

Do whatever it takes to make your data accessible to the rest of the company. Huge software companies like Tableau owe their very existence to this concept.

> Data is an important asset. Many of your colleagues— across many departments— need access to it.

Tableau's service provides an intuitive way to plug into any data source and generate graphs, reports, and CSV dumps. Data is only useful if you can extract and make sense of it. Large companies will have teams dedicated to data accessibility. If such a team doesn't exist where you work, then there's room for you to implement something!

Design Patterns

Injecting software design patterns into your team's routine is a double-edged sword that has the potential to be a high-leverage task. Patterns give consistent answers to questions like how to implement certain features, and they can neatly organize your software. However, they can also be areas of contention if other people aren't committed to following the patterns.

For ninety percent of software use-cases, existing patterns solve existing problems. For example, many people hate on Ruby on Rails, but I enjoy it. It may not be the most performant, it may not be the trendiest, but it is simple and it works. Ruby on Rails has well-defined patterns to help you implement web applications. As long as you're not expecting Facebook-level traffic, Rails is a great solution for many small to medium-sized projects. The framework is a strong solution because it defines simple, re-usable design patterns. No matter what feature you're implementing, if you follow the Rails convention, everyone on the team will understand your work.

Let's imagine that you have been assigned to implement a standard-protocol email authentication flow. Nothing fancy, a simple feature with a simple implementation. If you hold dearly to your personal preferences and refuse to adopt the Rails design patterns, performing a custom implementation would be a selfish act on your part—you've just sacrificed longevity and readability for ego.

There will be times that call for custom implementations. This is when no existing Rails design pattern fits the spec. These scenarios are rare, but they will happen and there's no reason to force convention on an unconventional situation—a custom problem warrants a custom solution.

Understand Neighboring Applications

When an application you're working on has neighbors, other applications and services that have a direct dependency on yours, it's easy to bury your head in the sand and treat them as someone else's problem. Do not do yourself and your neighbors this disservice. While it might be unreasonable to expect a Google programmer to understand the company's entire technical landscape, I would highly recommend that you do your utmost to understand the neighboring software around you—do not silo your expertise.

Nevertheless, understanding the technical nuances— even at just an interface level— across applications will be a high-leverage activity.

If you work at a small company, the system will be small and you will have an in-depth knowledge of the various subcomponents. If you work at a larger company, there'll be too much technology for one person to track. In these scenarios, you must mentally encapsulate functionality into black boxes and trust the system. Nevertheless, understanding the technical nuances—even at just an interface level—across applications will be a high-leverage activity. You'll realize the fruits of your labor when it comes time to collaborate with other developers and teams. Armed with a solid understanding of their systems, you'll be able to architect something much more robust than if you had limited yourself by hiding in your cave.

Conclusion

For any assignment, always ask yourself the two high-leverage questions: Does this benefit something bigger than me? Is this going to last a long time? Before you get too eager, remember that there will invariably be times when you're pinned down under a mountain of work. While there's no escaping coding crunch times, the best thing you can do is to periodically brainstorm ways to add leverage wherever you can. A quick document or a simple graph can go a long way. Soon, you will develop a sixth sense for leverage and you will easily uncover and make the most of it.

23: There Is No One-Size-Fits-All [Learning]

For people starting their journey into software development, the road can be daunting. There's a lot to learn, a lot of different ways to learn it, and a lot of end-game scenarios that you've painted for yourself. Many people at this level suffer from learning-paralysis. In their minds, they have created black-and-white paths for learning: *Should I take this Udemy course or this Coursera one?* As they become preoccupied with choosing the best path, they become indecisive with their actions.

If you've ever struggled with these kinds of choices, I can empathize; the number of courses, blogs, evangelists, and JavaScript frameworks makes my head explode too. If there's one thing to remember though, it's this—no matter what anyone claims, there will never be a one-size-fits-all plan for learning.

I've been asked countless questions about educational choices: *Should I major in computer science or computer engineering? Is Python better than Ruby? Is learning C worth it?* These questions are ultimately shortsighted and can pigeonhole you into a limited set of options that you have arbitrarily created for yourself. For example, let's consider this question—will learning C make you a better developer? If you're just trying to become technically literate, there is no reason to learn C. If you've decided you're going to get into enterprise software, then a quick Intro to C course wouldn't hurt,

...no matter what anyone claims, there will never be a one-size-fits-all plan for learning.

but you don't need to get into the weeds of bit shifting. If your end-game is to write device drivers or contribute to the Linux Kernel, then learning C is critical. Getting clarity in your long-term goals will enable you to ask yourself better short-term questions.

The tried-and-true way of learning is no secret—foundation. Elon Musk relates this to a tree. If you try to reach out to the branches without the tree having a strong trunk, you will fall. But if you develop fortified roots and a sturdy trunk, the branches you reach out to will be firm and steady.

Don't go off and learn about the nitty-gritty details of the latest web framework before you understand the basics of the Internet. Imagine a standard breadth-first-search. You start by performing a well-rounded foundation traversal. After one level, you dip your toes into some intermediate topics. Before going too deep, make sure you come back up a level to reinforce the basics—then dip your toes back into the deep end when you're ready. Before you know it, your baseline level will have elevated and you'll be conquering advanced topics. Perhaps this is how Elon Musk went from programmer to rocket-builder.

There will never be a silver-bullet path to learning, programming, dating, politics, or life. Be wary of the strong opinions of others; it is impossible for anyone to tell you what is best—there is no best language, there is no best framework, there is no all-or-nothing, there are no absolutes. Everything in life comes with pros and cons that you should judge for yourself. When you're

> *You will only frustrate and disappoint yourself if you believe in absolutes.*

a beginner and deciding how to learn, do not trap yourself with learning-paralysis. If you catch yourself looking for The Best Way, stop.

Keep your mind open and be receptive to different perspectives. Don't trick yourself into believing you need to learn one specific language. Learn as many as you want. Don't think you have to learn React because everyone else is. Try it out yourself and see if you like it over Angular. You will only frustrate and disappoint yourself if you believe in absolutes. This mindset is the root cause behind most of the questions I've received. I'm always happy to guide people through these questions, but the essence of my answer will never change. The answer is for you—and only you—to decide.

24: Your Boss [Career]

Throughout your career, you'll find yourself working under many different people. Some you may hate with a fiery passion, some you will show great deference to, and some you will consider to be incompetent.

If you end up with the perfect boss who respects you, is pleasant to work with, delegates wells, acts as a mentor, provides challenging work, pays you well, and looks out for you—then you have struck gold! For the individuals who truly have no boss, who own their own companies, owe no debts, and have shared no equity— this chapter might not be very relatable. For the rest of us, we answer and are responsible to someone else, and that person isn't always perfect.

Always Respect Your Boss

This has happened to me, my parents, and to all my developer friends at some point in our careers. There is always a boss who we believe to be a bumbling idiot. He or she has no insight into the code, isn't managerially or technically competent, and seems to have the easiest job in the world.

For some toxic organizations, these unfortunate situations may be a reality, but for the majority of cases, these feelings are rooted in your personal perspective. It's easy for us to judge someone based on the criteria of our own job rather than theirs. As a software developer, you cannot judge an engineering manager by their familiarity with the code—that's not their job.

Your position is no harder or more important than any another position; it is just a different one.

In any organization, each person has a unique role. There are people with boots on the ground and there are the middle managers overseeing execution. Directors manage big budgets, while executives play a game of thrones. Every position is important and has its own problems to deal with. Your position is no harder or more important than any another position; it is just a different one. Your boss's role in the company is different than yours. You *must* respect that.

It's easy to label someone incompetent if they don't know the ins and outs of *your* job. This is naïve and unfair. I've been guilty of this on numerous occasions, and when I've recounted my experiences to friends and family, they've all shared similar feelings. Catch yourself early if you're guilty of this.

Always Make Your Boss Look Good

As mentioned earlier, the vast majority of us answers to someone. You answer to your tech supervisor, who answers to a VP, who answers to the CEO, who answers to the board, who answer to the shareholders.

The lesson here is simple—if you make your boss look good by delivering great work, you make yourself look good. This will naturally make other people notice you and perceive you as a valuable asset—someone worth having on their team. At the end of the day, consistent high-quality work trumps playing politics and schmoozing. Making your boss look good not only builds value with your immediate team, but it builds value in the perspective of people around you—that is priceless. Write some good code for this project? You'll get asked to work on more important initiatives next year. Successfully manage and operate an engineering team? You'll get some VC's attention when you're looking for funding.

This simple premise carries through at every single level. Many people who are unmotivated at their current jobs immediately look towards other opportunities. This is a loser's mindset, a mentality that must be your last resort. Don't underestimate the leverage you can obtain—and the dollars you can earn—through solid, consistent work at your current position.

When you start feeling the pressures of demotivation, consider everything you can do to personally steer your own ship around. Your environment and your attitude are intimately related; you'd be surprised how things start to feel better just by keeping your mind positive. In the unfortunate scenario that you *really* need to look for other opportunities—perhaps to leave a toxic environment—then do so cordially, burn no bridges, and give your current position your all while you're still there.

No matter your situation, put in solid work, stay positive, and make your boss look good. Across the many chapters of your life, your good work and healthy attitude will accumulate, and this will inevitably lead to positive results.

Bring Up Issues & Maintain Tact

Your relationship with your boss will not always be sunshine and rainbows; you will have your fair share of disagreements and tension. In times like these, the manner in which you bring up issues is extremely important. Always maintain composure, tact, and discretion when bringing up your concerns. Many people underestimate how easy it is to create long-lasting bad will.

There are clear and common themes that arise in every work-based situation. All managers would love their employees to speak up more about their issues as soon as they occur. However, no one wants to have any issue laid at their feet in an emotional or unpleasant manner. If you have an issue, bring it up calmly rather than let your own frustrations and resentment get the better of you.

The average developer does not become disgruntled overnight. It takes a series of negative events that eventually snowball into a mountain of demotivation. This may be from too many mundane bug fixes, pointless refactoring efforts, bad chemistry with colleagues, or a loss of faith in the company. By the time the developer chooses

> *The average developer does not become disgruntled overnight. It takes a series of negative events that eventually snowball into a mountain of demotivation.*

to formally bring up these issues, they are biased and mentally exasperated. Suddenly company issues now feel like personal issues. Given these feelings, going into a potentially crucial conversation with your boss is a delicate interaction. Engineering managers can sense this almost immediately and can easily go on the defensive, rather than being the helpful senior team member you need.

As mentioned in the previous section, your relationship with your boss is special, and it is a relationship that must be nurtured. Issues will arise and you must bring them up quickly and respectfully. Do not wait until you are pulling your hair out before you call for a one-on-one.

Micromanagement & Consistency

Micromanagement is pervasive in any job. More often than not, when we reach the point where the word is used in the workplace, it's because something has gone wrong. Yet employees like to hand the blame to the boss—it's the boss who is paranoid, who is putting us under unwarranted scrutiny. If this feels like your way of thinking, take a step back and evaluate your own work. Are you producing at the same quality and pace you were a year ago?

Working fast or slow is fine, as long as you are consistently working fast or slow.

Managers increase scrutiny when someone's work has lost consistency. Consistency is a paramount for developers. Working fast or slow is fine, as long as you are consistently working fast or slow. This is why it is imperative you pace yourself. Having a high output for six months, only to slow down to a crawl for another six months, is reason for any manager to become concerned. Would they be doing their job properly if they were just to ignore the changes in your output? Without any additional information from you in the first place, what choice do they have?

25: Understand What You Are Doing [Coding]

Avoid at all costs any situation where you might find yourself unable to explain why your code is working. I cannot over-stress this; this is a developer's single most dangerous pitfall. Not being able to explain something that's broken is a simple matter of debugging, but not being able to explain something that's working is shooting yourself in the foot.

Understanding your code is a crucial part of your progression and effectiveness as a developer. For any modern project environment, there is a sea of beautiful frameworks and services providing plug-and-play magic to help you create masterful works of software art—all without you really needing to know how anything works. If you add in the right snippets from Stack Overflow and perform some selective copying and pasting, you'll be able to work your way through a majority of feature requests without really understanding what you've done.

Not being able to explain something that's broken is a simple matter of debugging, but not being able to explain something that's working is shooting yourself in the foot.

I've seen developers do this, and it can be frightening. Is this how you want to develop? I'm sure you already know the answer to that. We must strive to have total understanding of our work.

The Environment

Before diving into code, you will go through a standard environment setup process. During this time, you must understand exactly what is being configured and why. Sometimes you'll have a colleague sitting beside you who can explain what you don't get, while other times you might find yourself sifting through stale documentation. Whatever the case, give this process the attention it deserves. Your environment shouldn't be a mysterious black box.

If your team requires you to install some system packages, for example, ask yourself: What do they do? What files are installed? How do those scripts alter your environment? What do you do if it can't install the packages you need? Do you need to build anything from source? Take an inventory of all the unique processes that need to be running—MySQL, Redis, Rabbit, etc. If a script starts up twelve different Docker containers, understand at a high level why you need each one.

Familiarize yourself with whatever platform your colleagues have chosen for development. This is extremely straightforward, yet some people neglect to spend the appropriate amount of time doing exactly that. If your whole team is on Ubuntu but you've been using Fedora for the past five years, make the transition! A few jobs ago, my team had mandated a custom CentOS image that all the developers were supposed to use. A rogue developer refused to use CentOS and did all his development with Ubuntu. I shouldn't have to state the obvious, but it was painful for everyone.

Once your local is up and ready for development, you should know exactly what's running, why it's running, and every single step it took to get it there.

The Build Process

Every project is organized, interpreted, and built in a different way. After setting up your computer's environment, you'll do whatever it takes—no doubt with some help—to get the project ready for development.

> *Control over the application code is a no-brainer, but control over the build system will give you a leg up and pay dividends.*

Periodically take a pass at the build system to *really* understand how everything comes together. You must understand all the nuances and weird dependencies. Why is the directory structure laid out the way it is? How is third-party code getting integrated into the project? Do you know each and every step of the build? What subset of these steps can you get away with not running and why?

This build and configure process is pervasive across software development—every project has a layer of configuration surrounding its raw application code. This ranges from tricky CMake files with cross-platform compilation clauses, to obscure Webpack configuration flows that only the original author really understands. Do your best to learn about all of them; this will give you control over your project. Control over the application code is a no-brainer, but control over the build system will give you a leg up and pay dividends.

Debugging

Debugging is the best way to understand application flow. Breakpoints are your friends, and you can step, step, step your way into becoming a source-code master with them. If you're completely stuck, starting with main() always works.

You should never scrub through a sea of source files. This is a waste of time. Debugging will get you up to speed quickly and direct you to the specific files that you need to understand. Execute the code before understanding the source; you'll be in for a rough time if you do this the other way around.

Testing

For any reasonably-maintained project, there will be some level of testing—you deserve to flip a table right out of the room if there is none. Understanding how tests are structured is another essential part of development. The reasons are similar to why we must understand the build process—control.

Every project will be tested differently, but there are a few common themes. First, there's always some kind of scaffolding to set up test data. This could be a static file that loads a bunch of objects into memory before the suite is run, or a dedicated test database that you need to pull from periodically. Whatever it is, where there are tests, there's data.

Second, tests will likely include mocks for first-party and third-party services. In a world where people love abusing micro-services and paying for SaaS, we make an overwhelming amount of external calls, receive fancy web-hooks, or subscribe to a mashup of publishers. It can be difficult to keep track of what's ours and what's not. When looking through the source, understand which paths are real and which paths lead to mocked interfaces. What code are you actually testing? Do the mocks make sense?

Finally, don't spend too much time trying to understand other people's test code—it's going to look ugly. Not many people care how their tests are written, just as long as they're written. While you shouldn't really skimp on your test code, it doesn't have to be as pristine as application code. The minimum requirement here is that you have the tools you need to test, and that you actually *write* them. Testing is an amazing habit to get into and it will spur you on to write better software and become a better developer. As a professor once told me, every line of untested code is debt!

Deployment

Every single project is deployed somewhere. If you're writing a Linux library, you'll generate artifacts, package them into some special binary, and publish it to a repository. If you're working on a web application, you'll have to update code, migrate data schemas, and restart processes in project-specific ways on remote servers. Deployment is an intense process! Imagine the processes Netflix goes through to deploy new code and stay online at the same time, just so all of us can continue binge-watching TV shows—it's amazing!

For large software teams, deployment may be out of your scope, or it could be the only thing you work on. For smaller teams, understanding the deployment procedure is a necessity. Do your best to understand how code gets packaged up and sent to its final destination.

Neighbors

Last but not least, put in the effort to understand neighboring applications. No matter how many things you're working on, I guarantee there are a hundred more processes, micro-services, and applications that make the machine tick.

Whatever the context, understand your relationship with your direct neighbors. I use the word *neighbor* to mean any other internal application that your application depends on, or vice versa. How is data exchanged? Where are the interfaces defined? What is your application really responsible for? What is the communication medium between micro-services? You don't have to go as far as the neighbor's neighbors, but I won't stop you.

The end goal of this effort is to strengthen your grasp on the system. You may not understand everything, but you'll understand a whole lot more than if you remained working in a single-application bubble.

Every company packages their product up with a shiny bow, but if you take a peek under the wrapping, you quickly realize that it's a chaotic zoo.

Conclusion

In the realms of software, there are a ton of moving pieces that somehow end up working together. Every company packages their product up with a shiny bow, but if you take a peek under the wrapping, you quickly realize that it's a chaotic zoo. You *must* put in the effort to understand what you are doing at all times. As you can tell, this is significantly more than just understanding what you're coding. Don't just understand how *your* project is working, but strive to understand how *everything* works. It's going to be extremely challenging, but that's the fun part—right?

26: Red Flags When You Interview [Career]

Significant career decisions are pivotal moments in everyone's life. A decision almost all of us will face, at some point, is whether or not we sign the dotted line at the bottom of a job offer. Whether it's your first job or your fifth transition, interviewing and accepting a position are always important moments.

> Even though hiring managers are professionally trained recruiters, they're still human; they can still fumble from time to time.

Anyone who's transitioned can relate to that moment when you awkwardly excuse yourself to go to a "doctor's appointment" and slip out for an on-site interview. Everyone can relate to that first twinge of guilt when you start returning intro phone calls from recruiters.

Whatever the situation, you will inevitably find yourself in all kinds of emotional mind-states as you hunt down your first position or make up your mind to jump ship for a new opportunity. This chapter focuses on certain red flags that are good to keep an eye out for while job hunting. These are stressful times. You must stay focused to prevent yourself from making irrational decisions.

Strange Questions

Even though hiring managers are professionally trained recruiters, they're still human; they can still fumble from time to time. A few years ago, I was speaking with an HR representative at the tail-end of an on-site, when he asked how long I intended to stay with the company if I got the job. *What the heck?!* At that precise moment, the question didn't faze me—I was so eager to leave my old job that I brushed it aside without a second thought. This question was outrageous by even the most conservative standards.

Asking how long you intend to work for a prospective employer implies many things—never brush off a question like this. On the surface, this is a blunt and unprofessional way of checking your loyalty. Why would they ask this? If it's because you've changed jobs every six months, then it's a reasonable question. However, if it's because the engineers at their company are churning and turnover is at an all-time high, then alarm bells should ring. You might just have pulled back the covers on something you weren't meant to see.

This question is equivalent to asking someone on your very first date how many years they think you should date before breaking up—ridiculous! My advice here is to stay alert, scrutinize every question, and never brush something like this under the rug. If any question or apparently small remark seems off, there is an underlying backstory to it that can unearth useful insights.

Transparency & Integrity Check

Transparency from you is expected, but don't forget that you as interviewee can expect the same kind of transparency back from your interviewer. A transparent interview will feel genuine, honest, and like nothing is being held back. Are all your questions being answered thoroughly and to your satisfaction? Does it feel like anything is being purposefully hidden from you? Is anything being over-sold or over-represented? How would you measure the integrity of your potential employer? Pay attention to *how* things are presented to you, not just what's presented.

Excessive Salesmanship

You've spent the last two weeks showing off your coding chops and dominating the interviews. You've proven your worth, and now the company gears up into sales mode in its last pitch to bring you on board. At this stage of the game, you must keep an eye out for excessive salesmanship.

Some people are natural salesmen. You immediately like them, you nod your head more when you're with them, and they just make you feel comfortable. A good salesperson can sell practically anything to anyone; it's never about what they are selling, but about how you perceive them as a person.

The reality is that the whole world runs off of salesmanship and deals.

These traits are characteristics of many CEOs—it's one of the reasons they're in those positions in the first place; they've sold their idea to investors and they've sold their dream to employees. They might be selling to you right now!

My goal here isn't to paint sales in a negative light, but to remind you to remain vigilant when you are being sold to. The reality is that the whole world runs off of salesmanship and deals. Everything, from the small contract you sign with Verizon, to the most recent billion-dollar company acquisition, is a sales contract between two parties, at the end of the day. There is nothing wrong with salesmanship; you just need be aware of when and why it's happening.

When you're considering the possibility of a new job, be extremely specific with your questions. You and your potential employer will collaboratively uncover—with high integrity—the true nature of the position. If it's what you want, then the position should sell itself. Specificity begets honesty and will disable any salesmen from speaking at overly generic levels. Excessive high-level rhetoric is an immediate red flag.

Office Interaction Check

When you're on-site for an interview, make a mental note with regards to how people interact around that office. What's the vibe like around the water cooler? Do people look lively, or demotivated? Most likely, you won't be able to directly observe this, but even the smallest intuition can go a long way. Treat it like body language—the office's body language can carry significant weight in your decision.

More importantly, pay attention to the interactions with your interviewers. Evaluate how your interviewers describe their role, their work, and the company itself. When you ask, "What do you do on a typical day?" how enthusiastic are their answers? Do they care?

When the Interviewer Speaks Ill About the Job

This may seem like a no-brainer, but it happens more often than you'd think. I've been asked by an interviewer if I was sure I wanted to work there. This is a polite way of saying:

"Do not take this job! Get out of here ASAP!"

If an interviewer is going out of their way to drop hints like this, something is up—pay attention.

It's an experience both my friends and I have all been through, and it has consistently led us to unfortunate circumstances. When this happened to me, it threw me off—just not enough. I brushed off the remark as an insignificant hiccup and took the job anyway, because of the nice salary. It wasn't long before I realized I had made a terrible decision. That was a year and a half of unnecessary stress I will never get back.

While job hunting, it's convenient to turn a blind eye to the small quirks. You might be desperate, you might be putting your perfect company on a pedestal, or you might be prematurely honeymooning after a hard sell. Stay vigilant at all times. Patiently and objectively think about every interaction and every detail—obvious red flags might be staring you in the face.

Pay attention to your immediate feelings—especially the negative ones—and you will guard yourself from unfortunate circumstances and stress.

Listen to Your Gut

When it comes to job hunting, channel the stereotypical TV detective and listen to your gut. Your gut will know when you fit into the company culture. It will know how much integrity the CEO has while selling you the dream. It will know when your interviewer doesn't really like their job, even though they're trying to hide it. Pay attention to your immediate feelings—especially the negative ones—and you will guard yourself from unfortunate circumstances and stress. Career decisions are important decisions; your working life depends on them.

27: Setting Expectations Clearly [Stories]

Jessica and I had met and become friends at a budding startup. We were a consumer-focused startup with the lofty goal of building a next-generation web browsing experience on mobile. We liked native applications. We didn't like cramped, under-optimized webpages where we had to zoom in to click on radio buttons. The mission was to reinvent mobile web browsing and have customers choose us over Chrome, Opera, and the like. The bar had been set high, the undertaking was daunting, but it was enough motivation to inspire a strong team—just another day with your average startup.

For consumer-based startups, the game plan was pretty simple—raise cash, build something, and get people to download it.

So how does a young company go about attempting something like this? For consumer-based startups, the game plan was pretty simple—raise cash, build something, and get people to download it. We didn't have to worry about operations or fine-tuning our sales pipeline, we just needed people to download our app and give us five-star reviews. Money would come after popularity—the commonly held belief at the time. It's a gross over-simplification, but that's more or less how it went with many startups.

Jessica and I were part of the initial batch of developer hires. Right after the startup had raised its goal capital, they hired eight to ten engineers within a few months. Headcount tripled and we were off to the races. Jessica started a couple weeks after me, and we quickly developed a rapport.

We develop strong bonds with the people hustling beside us in the trenches. The ones who burn the midnight oil with us as we step through buggy code; the ones who hover over our desks waiting to press the release button. The person we can ask any question, with a single swivel of our chair. It's the only other person reading through our pull requests. There's something about writing a few hundred thousand lines of code together that fosters friendships.

My relationship with Jessica was built on our mutual respect for each other as developers. I can be a judgmental person, and I happen to be especially harsh when it comes to other developers' abilities. Of course, I keep these feelings to myself and always maintain diplomacy, but deep down I know who's good, who's so-so, and who's firing shots in the dark. I know where I fit in the grand scheme; I'm not your level 100 wizard programmer. I can take in requirements, produce solid code, and get the job done up to spec, but you won't find me writing compilers in my spare time.

Anyway, once the developer hiring wave had settled down, Jessica stood out immediately. I could tell by her communication, programming skills, and intuition that she was no stranger to the game. She saw the same in me, and a developer-to-developer mutual respect engendered our friendship.

As the ground troops of the operation, our lives were simple. We had a CTO, a VP of Engineering (VPoE), and other standard-protocol startup roles. The only thing we lacked was a product person, a void that would ultimately kill the company. Product development doesn't run smoothly when the CEO, designers, and developers all have an opinion and there isn't anyone laying down the law. Life as an "Individual Contributor" was simple. Jessica and I attended the same meetings, worked in the same code, and talked developer talk whenever we got a breather.

Fast-forward a year and a half to when the company was in trouble. We'd gone from working behind closed doors, with big ideas and bigger dreams, to the reality of life as a post-launch startup. Product iterations weren't improving traction, and a major pivot was slowly killing employee motivation.

During this time, I made the personal decision to leave the company and move on. Even though our tech never reached the level we were hoping for, this was a special experience for me because of the people. I had learned tremendous amounts, made new friends, and fulfilled my urge to see what startups were like. I was sad

I wasn't going to be able to work with Jessica any longer, but we wished each other well and made sure to grab dinner often.

Luckily for me, it didn't take too long to find something else, with a business-centric startup looking to start building out its software. Their engineering team only had two people—my old undergraduate roommate and one other remote developer. This startup was drastically different from the last. This was a business-to-business, service-based company that already had a customer base and growing revenue. This is no easy feat. Most startups will bleed one hundred percent of their VC money in an effort to create the next Instagram. The roots of this company were in sales and operations rather than engineering. They were able to make money before actually building any software.

That was an amazing sell for me, a developer coming from environments where engineering reigned supreme. I wanted to develop practical business and operational skills, instead of praying for downloads. Furthermore, since things were just starting out on the technical end, I would be able to design and implement a whole system from scratch—I had only worked on compartmentalized areas of the stack up to this point. This was an opportunity to give my technical and non-technical skills a major speed boost, and it delivered on all fronts.

The job description was simple—come in, figure out how the tech complements the business, and facilitate the company's growth into new markets. Also, let's not forget the most important part: write a ton of code. I was excited about the engineering journey and was looking forward to a deeper dive into financing, accounting, marketing, and other disciplines.

Since the company was so small, structure had not been established for any of the departments; it was just a group of people getting stuff done. My old roommate, who recruited me, had only started six months prior. The expectation was that we would be responsible for leading and growing the team. A definitive technical leader hadn't been established, but the CEO was hoping that my friend and I, leveraging our friendship and relationship, would grow the engineering department from the ground up.

Fast-forward to a year later. Our technical system had been growing day by day, and it felt like I had received an associate's degree in accounting and sales. The company was running lean, holding off until cash flow could break even before turning to any new venture capital. We were still only three developers and were stretched thin trying to help all the other departments.

Pretty soon, we realized that our bandwidth no longer matched our timeline and goals—we needed to get more programmers onboard and start prepping for expansion. I was impressed at how much we had accomplished up to that point, but there's only so much that three people can physically do. We began to plan for the difficult process of recruitment.

The first person I thought about recruiting was Jessica. It turned out that the timing was perfect. Jessica had been slugging it out at the same job for a year, but that old startup was finally deciding to close up shop. It was an opportune moment to put on my sales-hat and pitch her on my current company. Jessica and I had kept in touch ever since I'd left, she'd been giving me play-by-plays on random interviews with random companies, and I knew that nothing had peaked her interest. She had high standards and a good nose for bull. Jessica was talented, she was on the market, and I was excited at the thought of working with her again.

I pitched the company, telling her about how it was poised to expand and how we were already making money. We had all the other departments covered—marketing, sales, operations, finance, and product. I told her we had the bread and butter of a real company; this wasn't going to be a group of twenty engineers burning VC cash. We were sprinting to grow the tech, and we sorely needed her help. Fortunately, I had picked up a thing or two from my new friends in sales, and some of my persuasion techniques had leveled up. I got Jessica to come in for an official interview.

This is when the story takes a turn for the worse. During this courtship process, there was one important topic that I conveniently ignored—management—and that was a killer omission. At the time, we only had a vague idea of hierarchy within the engineering department. For the moment, the department was completely flat, and all three of us would meet weekly with our CEO and CFO for requirements gathering. Though it was not yet set it stone, I was under the impression that I would eventually begin reporting to my ex-roommate—he was, after all, the one who had recruited me. I also assumed that Jessica would eventually fall somewhere below me, since I was the one to recruit her.

> We were young developers who really had no idea how these things worked.

We were young developers who really had no idea how these things worked. We swept ticking time bombs under the carpet, and focused on sprinting and coding. The team would eventually fill out and everyone would fall into the right places, or so my ex-roommate and I thought.

But I was thinking only two steps ahead, when I should have been looking ten miles further. What if Jessica wasn't cool with reporting to me? I didn't know the answer to that because I hadn't asked. What if we were going to hire an external CTO one day? How important was rank to her? My mistake was my purposeful omission in place of an honest communication of our situation. Maybe that kind of stuff can fly with strangers, but it's a clear red-alert between friends. I told Jessica that the hierarchy wasn't yet established, but that there would be a need for leadership as our team filled out with more engineers. I did not at any time explain that she may well find herself reporting directly to me.

I wanted to recruit Jessica and bring her in on this golden opportunity. I held the company in high regard and wanted to share the journey. We needed someone with her coding skills, and I knew she wouldn't be on the market for long. We needed to get stuff done—I naively put the thorny issue of hierarchy on the back burner. I had expectations that I selectively left out of my sales pitch.

Now, for Jessica, management wasn't yet established, which meant she was on the same level as us—one of the ground troops—and had an equal opportunity to eventually climb into a leadership role. The idea that she would have to report to me had never occurred to her, due mainly to me failing to bring it up in our conversations.

I would quickly learn that having to report to me was a deal-breaker for Jessica. Perhaps it was because of our history as side-by-side developers, perhaps it was our friendship, perhaps she thought I was grossly incompetent, or perhaps it was just pure ego. I'll never truly know. All I know is that, as far as she was concerned, it was completely unacceptable to be under me on the company totem pole. This simple omission acted as the catalyst for months of stress and misery.

Jessica accepted the job offer and joined us in our cramped room with her new MacBook Pro. We were in a very different environment now. Remember, at our previous job we were in the trenches and things were simple. We got delegated work from the VPoE and we got it done—no drama. With this company, *we* were the engineering team responsible for making every single technical decision. Management came to us with their biggest problems, and we built solutions. This was high-level responsibility shared among us, without any indication of who was the technical leader.

With this level of open-endedness, things soon became complicated. We didn't always agree on the best direction to take with the software. With five departments asking us to build things, we didn't always agree about what was the most valuable thing to work on. This was compounded by the new dynamic we had as colleagues. I found myself having to guide Jessica through many non-technical aspects of the job, which was reasonable enough, given that I had been working there for almost a year. But I could tell she felt uncomfortable having me show her the ropes.

I was also behaving differently. Since I expected to step into a leadership role, I had begun acting as if that were already the case. Small things I did, which would have meant nothing if clear lines of authority had been established, got under Jessica's skin. I would ask her simple questions like whether she was enjoying her work, the kind of questions managers ask new staff, and would be met with the glazed eyes. My day-to-day peace of mind was taking a punch to the stomach, as I became evermore preoccupied with Jessica and our professional relationship.

Before long, it was blatantly obvious that things were not working out. I took it upon myself to try to fix them. I had hired Jessica; I was the one responsible for the problems. I had been trying to do this on my own for a while, but the issue was reaching breaking point. It was time to address the matter head on.

From an engineering execution point of view, we needed Jessica. Her coding skills were unreal; she had the potential to provide an insane amount of value. But our working relationship had broken down so much that it was affecting her work. To make things worse, I was right about the eventual managerial structure; I would report to my ex-roommate and Jessica would report to me, and this was about to become official. It was time to have a crucial conversation.

This single issue *was* the deal-breaker. By the time our scheduled meeting took place, Jessica already knew what was coming and had developed a resentment towards me—understandably. I tried to empathize with her anger; it was wrong of me to keep my expectations hidden from her when I sold her the job. Every time I opened my mouth, I could feel her discomfort.

Jessica ended up leaving the company. By the time this happened we had completely stopped hanging out. We had spent so much time and energy dealing with this problem at work that we had forgotten we were friends in the first place. The late nights grabbing dinner and drinks were over. This unfortunate professional drama had stained the friendship.

This took place over four long, arduous months. The root cause of it went all the way back to those days when I was pitching the company to Jessica as a friend and fellow coder. I should have made it crystal clear right then that she would probably be reporting to me, which would have enabled Jessica to make the most informed decision possible. If I had spoken openly back then, I have a hunch Jessica would have turned the offer down. I would rather have lost a coder than a friend, but what's done is done.

> *We had spent so much time and energy dealing with this problem at work that we had forgotten we were friends in the first place.*

This was painful learning experience for me. The smallest discrepancies can blow up in your face if they are left unaddressed. It was an honest mistake on my end, and it won't happen again. The best way to help others make an informed decision is if you lay all the cards out on the table beforehand.

28: Your Initiative [Learning]

There are only three stages of learning in life: what your parents teach you, what an institution teaches you, and what life teaches you. Being severely unqualified to talk about parenting, I'll move right on to the other two stages.

Learning in school is like night and day with real life's lessons. Academia is relatively easy. An iterated curriculum has been established and provided for you; you spend zero mental energy planning. All you need to do is follow the path given to you and pass the classes. This is table stakes, and you will be guaranteed intellectual growth.

A lot of my friends were surprised by how slowly they were learning after they left school; some even wanted to go back, just to have that academic rocket progression again.

When life hits, you suddenly have to plan your own curriculum, and this catches people off guard. A lot of my friends were surprised by how slowly they were learning after they left school; some even wanted to go back, just to have that academic rocket progression again. Whatever your situation, your learning will always be in your control—and it all starts with your initiative.

Opportunities to learn will be present for your whole life—as Henry Ford said, anyone who stops learning is old, whether at twenty or eighty. Anyone who keeps learning is young. For some of you, this may be a no-brainer. You might work at Google, where you can ingest huge amounts of information from qualified engineers on an almost daily basis. You might have an amazing mentor guiding you step-by-step through your career. You might be working on an amazing project where you're able to pick up a variety of new skills. If this sounds like you, feel free to skip this chapter—this is for everyone else.

There's a learning curve for any job. Once it plateaus, many people can turn on the cruise control as things get easy. Don't expect to get pushed hard by your performance reviews; they are most likely an inconvenience for your manager. At the end of the day, the only thing you have is your initiative; it has to be strong and it has to be a habit. I cannot instill this value into you, but I can show you its potential.

Asking

Asking is a very easy thing to do; it just needs to be done with a little bit of humility. There will always be someone more experienced than you, and it will be up to you to utilize that person's knowledge. Remember, this is your responsibility, not theirs. Your superior is not a soothsayer and will not be able to read your mind. They have the skills and experience; you have the honest introspection and self-awareness. Mix in some thoughtful questions, and you have a formula for growth. Simply asking, "How could I have implemented this better?" goes a long way.

Expertise Across Change

We change companies, departments, and positions throughout our careers. Each transition comes with new languages to learn, new frameworks to use, and more technical expertise to be gained. Change is an amazing growth catalyst, because it forces you to adapt to unfamiliar environments. Remember, you are a software developer—not a Python developer. You will learn any language and any stack to get the job done.

Let me share a quick story. Joe had been working with C++ throughout his entire professional career. He had memorized all the standard library interfaces, could recite all the Boost classes, and sometimes baked cakes with C++.

Each transition comes with new languages to learn, new frameworks to use, and more technical expertise to be gained.

Joe—who was working a comfortable job at JP Morgan—got sucked into the startup hype and moved to San Francisco to join a "fin-tech" unicorn. Life just turned upside down. Joe now had to move to Silicon Valley and start working with Java. Thinking Java was pretty much like C++, Joe initially floundered. Unconsciously, he thought he could carry his C++ knowledge as weight. C++ was raw, powerful, and more of a programmer's language. It would definitely be good enough for his new San Francisco job, he figured—yet it wasn't. Joe's supervisor eventually called him out and gave him the wakeup call to get his act together.

Joe had simply underestimated a new tech stack and failed to maintain his expertise across the transition. That wakeup call sent Joe diving deep into Java and its best practices. He now bakes cakes with multiple languages.

Do not make the mistake of assuming you have high credibility because you've developed across a few different stacks. Every company, technical stack, and development environment will be different. Once you transition, it's your responsibility to initiate your learning, ramp up, and become an expert again.

Mentorship

If you have someone you can call a mentor, take a moment and realize how lucky you are—then go give them a hug. For the other ninety-nine percent of us, we must find mentorship and guidance through other sources. The good news is that mentorship doesn't have to come directly from another human being. I've never been able to call someone a true mentor, but I've learned to fill that void with my own initiative.

Here are two amazing mentors that have helped me—books and YouTube. With books, find someone you respect, read their work, and immerse yourself in their brain. There are some incredible people in this world who have taken the time to write down their thoughts and experiences—take advantage of that!

My second mentor is YouTube and the Internet in general. These days, you can learn the fundamentals of any topic with just a few key strokes; not many people understand how incredible this is. Respect someone? I guarantee they have multiple documentaries and full-length interviews online. Want to sit in on an "elite" Stanford lecture? No problem, just watch it sped up at 1.5x after dinner.

If you don't have the luxury of a real-life mentor, don't worry, you are in the majority. With books, YouTube, and the Internet, there are more resources than we could ever hope to consume in a single lifetime. Everything is out there, you just need the initiative to get up and find it.

Non-Tech Makes A Difference

My last snippet of advice is that you should not limit your educational pursuits to just tech. The world is a big place, and everyone—really, everyone—has something unique to share with you. Learning about other industries and professions outside your field will increase your value as a software developer. You can read about basic accounting, learn how the healthcare industry works, read up on some politics, or try to understand human psychology. Anything you learn will complement your work as a technologist in some way, shape, or form.

Anything you learn will complement your work as a technologist in some way, shape, or form.

29: The Quickest Way Out [Stories]

The following story comes from a friend's experience starting a career with a wedding company based in New York. I was surprised to see how happy she was with her company's culture—a lot of my friends weren't so lucky. Her company was decisive and swift when hiring and firing. There were no qualms over letting the bad apples go. Her story demonstrates the significance of inter-personal skills and how an individual's conduct can trump ability.

Company culture has been a hot topic these past few years. We've seen a Google software developer's gender "manifesto" lead to his firing and a brave blog post spark the departure of Uber's CEO. While a lot of people talk about culture, no one defines it well. Every company believes in diversity—but so what? Every company has integrity as a value—so what?

> *A company is a group of people providing a product or service—that's it.*

Don't over-complicate the concept of a company. A company is a group of people providing a product or service—that's it. It's simple on the surface, but incredibly nuanced under the covers.

What is the most unique, dynamic, dramatic, and powerful thing in life? The answer is a group of people. That simple concept is the essence of humanity. It's how we define ourselves and ranges from companies, to towns, to countries. It was people who created the iPod and it's people who start wars. If we have to start somewhere with company culture, we have to start with the people.

Two years ago, I was a newly minted software developer and had started working at a medium-sized wedding startup. We were a one-stop-shop for couples tying the knot, providing services such as gift registries, invitation management, and photo album creation. Aside from the work itself, I'm proud to say that I thoroughly enjoyed working with everyone in the company. After a marathon of technical interviews, I was beginning to suspect that "just being nice" wasn't a common attribute for tech companies. Here, everyone was respectful and intelligent, and contributed to a pleasant work environment.

One of the hallmark traits of the company was a strict no-jerk policy. While in the rest of life I was used to just having to put up with tough personalities every now and then, this company was breaking records for shortest jerk-employee tenures.

During my first six months on the job, our team was on a roll. We were hiring at a steady clip, leveling up our tech, and pushing out product—all at the same time! We had picked up a couple of infrastructure engineers, a bunch of full-stack web developers, and two awesome product managers.

With many of our seasoned developers looking to stay inside the code, managerial duties weren't getting enough attention. Many of my colleagues had been managers in previous jobs and were now only interested in developing. For my first six months, we had been very lucky with our hires, but this luck led to a lack of scrutiny in recruitment. We met an engineering manager named Bob. He had the right qualifications and got along with everyone during the interviews. With confidence, our company gave him an offer.

Bob's tenure at our company lasted a little over two months. I don't believe Bob was a bad person, but a few recurring personality traits led to his swift removal. The one thing about him that I will always remember is that Bob was always critical, and never constructive. We noticed it immediately, as his criticism appeared every-where, from code review comments to architecture de-sign meetings. He was quick to veto proposals, point out flaws in the system, and push hard for his solutions. Two of his favorite phrases were "that's not going to work" and "I'll come up with a design." These might be acceptable traits for an enthusiastic devel-oper, but they were inexcus-able ones to find in a manager.

As an entry-level developer, I've noticed how often senior developers forget how challenging programming can be.

As an entry-level developer, I've noticed how often senior developers forget how challenging programming can be. I don't see all the nuances, edge-cases, and ripple effects like they do. I don't think they can reasonably expect me to, either. I'm aware that my design isn't winning any prestigious coding competitions, but a senior going off and architecting the system in a silo doesn't help me get any better.

I did not come from a formal engineering school. I was a Math major, took an interest in coding, signed up for a boot camp, and was lucky enough to get a developer job. I often feel that I do not have the thick skin that comes with the fancy Ivy League, Silicon Valley training. Because of this, perhaps, I've become perceptive of the various ways in which technical criticism is given.

Many developers are quick to point out exactly what's wrong and, without any discussion, provide a solution. I know this is extremely practical, but it's highly aggravating for any developer trying to formulate ideas. If I've written a crappy interface, I don't want to be told exactly what it should have been. Good technical criticism starts where solutions are lacking: "Hey, have you thought about how your interface can extend to our new features coming into the pipeline?" or "There seem to be a mix of responsibilities with another interface we have; is there a way to re-organize them?"

The trickiest part of being a team member in any company is interacting with the people. With coders coming from eclectic backgrounds, strong cultures and comfortable work environments take precedence over raw talent. I know the veterans mean well, but their devotion to the optimal solution might come at the cost of raising the team collectively. A seemingly innocent habit might be the deal breaker for a job.

30: Duress And Rationalization [Stories]

Dan, my first Qualcomm friend to join start-up-land at the tumultuous L.A. fitness company, is back with a story about career transitions. This chapter follows Dan as he closes a chapter and starts a new one in his startup journey. Learning about Dan's concerns and emotions during his career pivots has helped me tremendously over the years. We have shared many struggles over beers, and he has been an invaluable earpiece for me during my own pivots.

Leaving a company can be emotional. You might be leaving an intimate group of developers. You might be leaving a CEO who went out on a limb to hire you, or maybe you're disappointing your co-founder and soon-to-be ex-best-friend. You might be in love with your current job, but I promise you there will be a day when you come face to face with these difficult emotions. A company can be like a second family, and closing that chapter in your life is no easy task, but when you know it's over—it's over.

It was 2015, and I had been working at the L.A. fitness startup for a couple of years. The sexy idea for a fitness app was still high in the sky, but our future looked increasingly grim as the months passed by. Developers were churning, investors were wincing over our bug-crippled demos, and we had absolutely nothing to show in the numbers. I was struggling to keep up my motivation. The only thing keeping me onboard was my faith in the

A company can be like a second family, and closing that chapter in your life is no easy task, but when you know it's over—it's over.

CEO. As the days passed, my itch to leave only worsened. It didn't help to see our leader slowly losing his fire. After a few months of suppressing my emotions, I was ready to do whatever it took to get out of there. I was stressed, I wasn't in the right state of mind, and I made a major mistake. I left for the sake of leaving.

Looking back on those times, it's so clear to see what I did wrong. I can offer this simple tip for anyone in a similar situation: get a neutral third party to hear you out and weigh in with their thoughts. An objective mind is invaluable; use someone who has zero affiliation with the job or your own personal situation—no colleagues; no partners, husbands, wives or dependents; just someone who can listen to your issues and give an unbiased opinion.

Due to extreme impatience and stress, when another opportunity presented itself to me, I accepted it immediately. Hindsight will always be 20/20, and I want to smack my head against a wall every time I relive this decision. When I look back, it was obvious that I should never have taken that other job—the signals were clear, but I didn't acknowledge any of them. I made excuses to myself, rationalized away blatant red flags, and completely ignored my gut instincts.

The new company I ended up joining was co-founded by my college friend and headquartered in San Francisco. Before I was consumed by the failing L.A. fitness startup, this particular friend and I would periodically grab beers and I'd hear about all the craziness happening in his company. I heard about investors acting like bullies, friends becoming enemies, and day-to-day in-fighting among management. It was bar talk between friends. Said another way, this was a dialogue that a founder should never, ever have with one of his or her employees. During these bar sessions, I did my best to be understanding, but all I could think about was, *Your company sounds insane, man.* Unfortunately, by the time I accepted his offer, I had pruned these thoughts away. *It's completely normal for a startup to be chaotic.*

There were other major signals that I ignored. A year before this all started happening, I had introduced my younger brother—also a software developer—to my friend's company. Just when I was about to accept the job offer, my younger brother was planning to leave! Why would he be leaving? Was it because something was wrong with this company?

I never asked my brother why he left. In the back of my mind, I was scared, because I knew I wouldn't like what I'd find. Instead, I attributed his leaving to personal ambitions and assumed it had nothing to do with the company itself. My desire to leave the fitness startup was so strong that it overshadowed any rational thought. I had neglected to perform the much-needed diligence on this new company before jumping ship. To this day, I cannot believe I ignored these warning signs. My brother and I are the same blood. Why did we not talk about this? Why did I not get every ounce of truth out of him about that company?

Catch yourself quickly when you find yourself rationalizing away difficulties. This goes beyond your career and can touch everything in your life. Frequent justifications are a signal that your reasoning has been compromised. All you need to do is remember my story—I willingly joined a startup after hearing a boatload of negative gossip from its CEO, and I joined on the heels of my own brother leaving!

The rest of this story plays out as you might expect. I knew I had made a huge mistake as soon as I started. Every single crazy story I had heard over beers was now my reality. I spent just one year working there and it was rough.

> *Frequent justifications are a signal that your reasoning has been compromised.*

I joined shortly after a large Series B round of funding. For many Silicon Valley startups, this round is extremely significant. It is a huge injection of capital that is dedicated to growth. New positions form, teams start filling out, and power-jockeying sky rockets to an all-time high. Times like these offer many opportunities to employees. After years of grinding as a tiny company, it's no surprise that people are eager to step into bigger roles and have more influence. These are very delicate times; a bad outside hire or premature promotion of an old employee can seriously hurt the company. Suddenly, everyone—from every department—felt that it was now the appropriate time to start hiring and creating new teams underneath themselves. I could feel the anxiety; people wanted to get on the right rung of the ladder.

Obviously, this kind of situation doesn't happily resolve for everyone. To placate his employees, my friend—the CEO—started becoming very liberal with titles. All of a sudden, vice presidents began popping up everywhere. I'm no business management expert, but a top-heavy management hierarchy full of millennials didn't seem very reasonable. Soon, it felt like everyone was a director or VP of something.

With the injection of this new money, investors were now scrutinizing numbers. We had to hit revenue goals, and I could feel the stress building on top of the sales team. Slowly but surely, what they were selling started to stray away from what we actually had to offer. Sales reps were doing whatever it took to close the deal. Features were promised, solutions were oversold, and many customers were in for an unpleasant surprise. Our offering was a one-time-sale product. Since revenues were not recurring, the only thing that mattered was closing the deal.

You can imagine what followed—promises not matching up with reality is never a good look. I'll spare you any more details, but more startup absurdity ensued. If you're interested in more juicy stories, there's plenty of reading material out there on Silicon Valley. It's usually more fun to read about than to live through.

Every experience—no matter how bad it may seem—is a learning opportunity. Even though I might have wasted a year of my life, I was left with these lessons that I can share with you today. I can't help but feel a twinge of regret when I look back on this. If I had cleared my head in L.A., if I been patient, I could have steered my career in a better direction earlier. There are only so many career-changing moments in your life, and it stings when you realize you messed one up. But in the end, it's all about learning and progressing.

> *Every experience—no matter how bad it may seem—is a learning opportunity.*

If you're rationalizing away red flags, you need to smack yourself and take a breather. Never leave a company for the sake of leaving. Take your time with any decision that affects your life. Finally, don't dwell on your past blunders or your future prospects; keep your mind in the present and your thoughts will be clear.

31: Places You Can Work [Career]

Everyone's career path is unique. Whether you're an entrepreneur, gig freelancer, pig farmer, or full-time developer, the paths and milestones that comprise each career are vastly different. For some, a career is synonymous with life; for others, the delineation between business and pleasure is cut and dried. Whatever it may be, all of us have aspirations, at varying levels, for our professional lives.

This chapter is dedicated to a specific group of people—anyone looking for employment as a software developer. This group does not include starving founders, one-man consultant services, elite hackers, or professional gamers. Even though we've narrowed down the career options, employment as a software developer is still extremely broad and can be an intimidating maze of what-ifs.

> *For some, a career is synonymous with life; for others, the delineation between business and pleasure is cut and dried.*

One of the most crucial decisions you'll need to make is the seemingly simple choice of where to work. You already know the factors: life responsibilities, what tech you're trying to learn, how much money you're trying to make, or what group of people you're trying to help. All of the above will be resolved by your own internalization.

The finishing touch to your decision will revolve around a significant factor that's outside your control—the software job types that are out there.

Information Technology Vs. Software Development

Before getting started, let's discuss how IT is different than software development. It's an important distinction, but it confused me for many years. Every company needs an IT department, but not every company needs a software development department. I'll put money down on the claim that every company—every single company—uses computers. Goldman Sachs uses IT to set up floors and floors of computers for their stock traders. Your grandma's basement business uses a special family-plan IT—AKA you and your computer expertise—

Every company needs IT, but not every company needs software development.

to get her dusty computer online and upgraded out of Windows 95. If your company uses computers, you need Information Technology!

The local high school, nursing home, and construction company all need computers. They need someone to set them up, create logins, secure networks, check licenses, and deploy the software needed for people to do their jobs. A gross over-simplification, yes, but it's essentially what IT provides. Their goal is to set up the computer and network infrastructure, so the company can operate. They also write software on top of all of this, but it's purposeful and enables their primary operational goals.

Now, how is software development different? The purpose of a software development team is *not* for internal infrastructure. The goal of a software team is to create a unique technical product, or service, for the company. Google has thousands of software teams working on fancy products like Google Plus, but they still have a dedicated IT team to handle their internals. Compare that to your local college; they probably don't need a software development team, but they definitely need someone to maintain all the student email accounts.

When you think about IT, think about infrastructure and plumbing. When you think about software development, think about applications and services. Software development is building something novel, iterating on it, and selling it for money. You can even build software that helps facilitate IT—Google Apps for example. Every company needs IT, but not every company needs software development.

Startups

In my humble opinion, there are only three categories of startups. They don't fall into industry or sector groups, but are singled out for the experience offered.

The first experience available comes to those starting their own company as founders. Founding a company is an enormous undertaking and responsibility, a topic that is far beyond the scope of this book and my own personal career path. If it interests you, there are countless testimonials, interviews, and books from founders kind enough to share their journeys with the world, and I wholeheartedly encourage you to seek out their stories.

The second experience is becoming a developer for a tiny startup. At this stage in the game, the startup is very high-risk and has much to prove. You'll be pumping out code to make that first splash onto the scene or hustling door-to-door to make those first dollars. These developer roles are primed for cowboy types who love green pastures and writing code from the bottom up. This level of startup is optimized for a jack-of-all-trades experience and can make for great, accelerated learning venues. For some, this environment is something to dabble in, just to see how wild the ride is.

The term "startup" represent two things— finding the mysterious product-market fit and being able to successfully repeat it at a non-trivial scale.

For others, it's something to avoid at all costs. And for a small minority, it's an addictive experience they'll want repeat many times over.

Finally, the third experience is working at a growing startup. At this stage of the game, the product or service has been vetted and the obstacle is now replication and execution. The startup has raised a healthy chunk of capital that has been earmarked for growth and expansion.

This experience is optimized for those who want to be part of a budding engineering department—this is not a pristine green pasture for cowboys. Process must be established, management becomes a real thing, drama escalates, and technical specialties start becoming delineated.

Anything beyond this level I do not consider a startup. The term "startup" represent two things—finding the mysterious product-market fit and being able to successfully repeat it at a non-trivial scale. Anything after that is a private company.

Private Company

A private company is what startups aspire to be. At the time of writing, some examples include Airbnb, Uber, and Patagonia. These companies are not startups; they are operating companies that aren't traded on the public stock market.

This stage of a company's life cycle is defined by many unique circumstances. If a company wants to liquidate, or is strapped for cash, it might file for an Initial Public Offering (IPO) to go public. Some private companies might plan for an acquisition. Other companies like Patagonia—a very successful outdoor clothing company—may choose to stay private indefinitely for personal reasons. The company's finances, execution aptitude, the energy of its founders, and various other circumstances will influence how long it stays private.

When a company has reached this point in its growth, the engineering experience has been formalized. You will be assigned to a team, have a well-documented work-flow, and be a part of the machine. Your task load will be lighter than what you'd expect at a startup. The work assigned to you comes after much deliberation, and there is zero room for cowboys. Many developers who enjoy the do-it-all lifestyle of pumping out two thousand lines of code a day will become bored at this level. The cowboys usually leave to find their next green pasture, moving away from the "official" engineering process.

Big Tech Company

These are the big players you already know about. They are billion-dollar publicly traded companies that have become household names—Amazon, Microsoft, Facebook, Google, Apple. You'll have a brand to put on your résumé, a huge networking pool, and access to all the world's resources. Three-

While the company might be known for working on cutting-edge technologies, you might be working on maintaining a couple of buttons.

hundred-thousand-dollar yearly license for a single piece of software, just because you feel like it? No problem. You'll be surrounded by smart people, achieve steady career advancement, see your bank account grow, and live a very comfortable life. You'll become a cog in the machine, but the machine can be an enjoyable place.

Join a big company when you understand exactly what it will provide you. While the company might be known for working on cutting-edge technologies, you might be working on maintaining a couple of buttons. If your only job was to make sure the Facebook settings page stayed up to date, would you be satisfied with that work? Huge companies are not places for the extremely ambitious. They are places for brand, networking, comfort, and cash. These are all great things—just make sure you know what you're getting into.

Big Company / Enterprise

These are gigantic, publicly traded companies that are not primarily tech. As a catch-all phrase, I'll represent them with the term "enterprise." Examples include Avis Car Rental, Walmart, Marriot Hotels, and Mount Sinai Hospitals. These companies provide products and services that aren't technical in nature, but that doesn't mean they don't need technical expertise; I guarantee a hospital needs serious IT and programming to service all its patients! These billion-dollar entities need software developers, but their goal isn't to build rocket ships to land on Mars.

Enterprises carry many of the same characteristics as the big tech players. You'll have brand recognition, resources, and a cozy life; you just won't be associated with the tech world. For the true tech companies—Tesla, SpaceX, Akamai—working as an engineer there will automatically label you as extremely technical. Programming for Nike won't exude the same impression. In reality, the Nike developer could easily be just as skillful, if not more so, than the Tesla developer. However, we shouldn't dismiss the general perception with regards to the companies you have worked for—the branding is important.

Finally, another major benefit of enterprise employment is the exposure to various non-technical business aspects. Working at Walmart exposes you to supply-chain management. Working at Marriot Hotels exposes you to the hospitality industry. Working at Goldman Sachs exposes you to finance. There is a lot to be learned outside tech, but you won't be exposed to these parts of life inside a research lab. Whether you're a technical purist or a jack-of-all-trades polyglot, pick and choose based on your personal preference.

Consulting

Consulting covers a broad spectrum that is tied to the idea of established experts lending out their knowledge. I've bucketed consulting firms into two major categories: those who implement, and those who do not.

If no implementation is involved, there will be little need for actual coding. These consultants operate at a high level and employ experienced technologists to give a bird's-eye view of strategy. This can range from system design, to architecture review, to formulating a technical grand vision.

If you work for a consulting company whose staff advertise themselves as "implementers," on the other hand, you'll need to engage in heavy amounts of building. Clients will come and go, and you will provide both expertise and solutions. Once you're done, the clients own what you've developed.

I recommend this avenue to anyone who is technically seasoned and confident providing a high level of expertise to others. I will issue a warning to those who are considering consulting and are still early in their careers. Many of my peers found jobs at large consulting firms, but due to their inexperience, they merely offered pre-meditated solutions that were handed to them by the company. There wasn't much thinking involved.

Agencies

Agencies are similar to consulting firms, but with a subtle twist—they are not expected to transfer knowledge or deliver abstract solution-building. The client relationship is extremely clear—we are hiring you to build something very specific, for a price, by a certain date.

Agencies often specialize in specific platforms or frameworks. There are agencies that specialize in mobile development and others that specialize in desktop software, for example.

Join an agency if you enjoy sprinting. You will spend six months building a new iOS application for Starbucks, then quickly move on to the next big thing. It might feel empowering to be writing an application for Starbucks, but don't feel too special—Starbucks employs many agencies to build different versions of their apps.

Join an agency if you don't mind rapid turnover. You must feel no attachment to your code, because in the end, you own none of it. Top-line revenue dollars will always take priority over code quality; there is no refactoring and there is no cleaning up the technical debt.

Finally, join an agency if you don't mind inconsistency. The lifestyle of agency employment is highly preferential to the people who bring in the cash. If you're lucky enough to be on the team that lands the big Disney contract, you'll be treated like a rock star and get the expensive standing desk you requested. If your department is running on a dry spell and isn't working on the big-ticket items, then your work—and the way you are treated—will quickly become dull.

Government

Another popular place for software developers to work is in the government. When I was eighteen, I remember the NSA and FBI had booths at our school's job fair. I applied for an internship with the NSA, and they asked me to fill out a ten-year background check—just in case I was doing anything sinister at age eight!

The gist of government work is simple. It's highly technical, but agonizingly slow. You will be working on jets, missiles, and radar. You will be writing real-time,

> *The gist of government work is simple. It's highly technical, but agonizingly slow.*

high-performant, meticulously-tested software to make sure the government can do whatever the government wants to do.

There are two main avenues for this line of work. You either work directly for the government, or you work for companies that land huge government contracts. In the U.S., some examples include Boeing, Raytheon, and Lockheed Martin. These are publicly traded companies which receive most of their work and cash from the government. The contracts usually read something like this: "Please build us a next-generation fighter jet and drone in the next five years. Here's five-hundred million dollars."

In the United States, a commitment to the government is no laughing matter. I know many people who've gotten Top Secret clearance in their twenties—think of Edward Snowden. Though Snowden is an extreme example of life taking some huge unexpected pivots, it serves as a reminder of how serious a government job can be. If you're suddenly handed top-secret information, what happens when you feel like looking for another job? I don't want to scare you, but just gently remind you of the gravity of these government positions. For these kind of jobs, there are many aspects to consider outside the technical.

Academic and Research & Development

Another job type for a select few is the highly academic ivory tower. These jobs exist in universities and research and development (R&D) centers within large corporations. You might be a professor pushing the limits of quantum computing or a computer science PhD working on new routing algorithms for Amazon.

The premise of an academic position is a special one. You and your team are inventors tasked with creating tomorrow's tech. Many of the technologies we take for granted today—desktop interfaces, LTE cellular, C—all came from R&D environments. Big tech companies invest a chunk of their capital into research, in hopes that their engineers will produce something that can eventually make the big bucks. Academic environments aren't bound by sprints, agile development, or definitive product cycles. They are slow, experimental, and have a degree of expected failure.

Academic positions will also vary widely between universities and huge companies. Working with a professor might entail fundraising, publishing stress, and frequent conference trips. I don't think there will be any cash problems if you work for Google X's research department.

The academic position is perfect for someone looking to tinker and shift their attention back and forth between new challenges. It is not for anyone yearning for operational execution. If you love shipping product and getting in front of customers, R&D won't fit. If you don't mind banging your head on tables and not thinking twice when your code gets scrapped, then R&D might be the perfect fit.

By Industry

Last, but not least, let's talk about the job type that isn't actually a job type. Unique experiences follow unique industries, and a software developer can be employed by any industry. Every industry you can think of—education, gaming, weddings, real estate, marine biology, clothing, partying, traveling—all need some form of code.

Considering the industry makes a significant difference when you have an affinity towards something particular. What do you love? Let's say you've been a serious gamer for the past fifteen years and you finally decide you can no longer spend every day, from dawn till dusk, wired on Red Bull. It might behoove you to follow the path of gaming and pursue the role of game developer—wouldn't working at Blizzard be a dream? Work touching our personal interests is extremely rare; take advantage of it if you can.

32: Simplicity [Coding]

In code and in life, we are told to "keep things simple." This little directive seems obvious, easy even, but fully ingraining it into your skills takes conscious effort.

Software systems are notorious for turning into complex behemoths. Give an innocent project five years, and it will make the bravest of developers cry a little inside. This aspect of software is undeniable, and it's one of the reasons classical-thinking engineers don't consider software to be pure engineering. A purist view of engineering will point you to bridges, cars, and skyscrapers. A design is established, the implementation steps are well-defined, and we end up with a well-oiled eight-cylinder engine. Software is *not* like this. Every aspect of software development lends itself to subjectivity and complexity—a million ways to do one thing, a constant churn of developers in and out of projects, perpetually changing business requirements, tight deadlines, third-party libraries becoming deprecated. The list is endless.

> *Give an innocent project five years, and it will make the bravest of developers cry a little inside.*

It is what it is—the nature of software-building will always be dynamic. To combat this flux, developers must make a consistent and sincere effort to simplify their code. This takes many forms, from periodic refactoring tasks to practical challenges to the status quo, but at the end of the day, every developer must value simplicity.

Reduction

Always look to make reductions. You don't need a hundred gadgets lying around collecting dust in your home, and you don't need to keep random interfaces and layers of indirection around in your software. Extra gadgets and useless code become attachments that weigh heavily; both life and code become much easier without them.

Reduce your code, but maintain its functionality. Is this feature completely deprecated? Make a sincere effort to truly deprecate it instead of just marking it as @Deprecated and forgetting about it. Is your solution a little preemptive? Don't include it yet! Stash it away and save it for later. Premature optimization and over-engineering should be familiar phrases.

Our code should do exactly what it needs to do—nothing more, nothing less.

As much as we love to add new code, deleting code can feel very therapeutic. Everyone loves to see a code review filled with red lines. Our code should do exactly what it needs to do—nothing more, nothing less.

Fixing Problems Doesn't Make it Better

It's easy to get caught up in day-to-day bug fixes and fires. If we fix problems, we feel pretty good about ourselves, but be careful—fixing problem after problem implies applying patch after patch to the codebase. Too often, we nonchalantly make change on top of change, feel content about iterative improvements, and move on with our day. If your team has been doing this, take a step back and ask yourself if fixing these problems is doing more harm than good. Chances are that you are introducing more complexities into the system, which will get in your way further down the road.

Challenge the Fundamentals

In order to simplify the system, you must challenge the fundamentals. Every software system has a custom foundation—this may be five very important classes, a specialized protocol, a colossal database table, or perhaps just a special way of writing files. You might have written this foundation yourself or merely inherited it. You start to notice that for every change introduced and for every problem fixed, you and your team rely on this foundation to behave like it always has. After long periods of time, this foundation becomes set in stone inside the company's software and becomes increasingly intimidating for anyone to change.

None of us are fortune tellers; we can't guess our future requirements or predict what our clients will demand of us in the next year. It's impossible to build a system that is flexible enough to withstand every use-case with ease. There will invariably come a time when you'll be faced with some difficult implementation decisions.

Should you really introduce that hacky code path? Should you really just add a bunch of columns to this colossal table? Remember, nothing is impossible! What if you challenged the fundamental building blocks? What if you could change something in those five classes or those shared interfaces? What if you could split apart that insane table or the monolithic Mongo collection?

The benefit of such work is hard to fathom for people outside of the software. Company executives and management will be reluctant to spend hundreds of engineering hours on something that seemingly pro-vides no value. You can't blame them; technical debt is hard for anyone to measure who isn't familiar with the code. Nevertheless, it's up to you—the developer—to be the biggest proponent of the company's code. It's al-ways possible for the foundation to change, and it may be one of the most significant initiatives that the compa-ny will ever pursue. Hundreds of hours spent this month might save thousands of hours next year!

Primitive Rules

I'm constantly amazed by the raw power of primitive building blocks. Sprawling Minecraft cities are construct-ed with stackable rectangles, complex space theories are formulated from simple laws of physics, and a bunch of transistors and electricity can give us smartphones.

This is the magical part of technology. Every layer of tech—from hardware to software—encapsulates away the details and provides shiny interfaces for its users. Stack a collection of these layers together and you can create mind-blowing systems. In order for a system to scale and change the world, its citizens must abide to a set of primitive rules. Consider the Internet—follow its rules and you gain access to a global network, reach billions of people, and store an infinite amount of data. Whether it's your computer, your phone, your refrigera-tor, or even your smart-mattress, it can get online as long as it follows the basic rules of the Internet.

A microcosm of this idea lies within the codebases that we work inside during our day-to-day. The software we craft is miniscule compared to the Internet, but it's still a complex world that we've constructed. What kind of primitive rules can we establish for our software? Perhaps a strict set of interfaces must be adhered to, or maybe a complex network acknowledgment protocol must be established. Outside of software, you can also establish rules around process. Post-mortems to complete after outages or methods of managing tech debt can be great things for the team. Primitive rules can help anywhere.

I want to issue a warning to everyone. Many of your colleagues will brush off these ideas as trivial when you first introduce them. The nature of primitive rules is that they are extremely simple; other developers will inevitably label them as unnecessary procedure. Don't let this deter you! Spend some time brainstorming these rules for your software. Always remember that it's the simple rules that enable the mind-blowing systems.

33: Feeling Left Behind [Career]

One of the most pervasive sentiments for software developers is the feeling that they've been left behind by the tech industry. I received an email from a software developer in India who had been working for IBM for four years. The general tone of the email was one of anxiety; the developer was worried he wasn't keeping his skills up to date and was stressed out from working with a codebase that dated to 1995. This chapter is a breakdown of that email.

Working on Irrelevant Tech and Falling Behind

The unfortunate news is that if you're not careful, you *will* get left behind, becoming less desirable to employers, and have anxiety flood your veins. Find solace in the fact that you are not alone; millions of developers around the world face the very same challenges.

It's a balancing act keeping yourself up to date—periodically picking up new skills is a must, but you don't need to hop on the bandwagon of every new web framework. However, if you do absolutely nothing—if you pick up zero new languages and refuse to try anything new—then of course you will fall behind. Imagine trying to go against the direction of a moving sidewalk at the airport: sprint and you get ahead, walk and you stay in place, stand still and you fall behind.

You need to make a judgement call on how close you stay to tech's latest and greatest. This call is yours to make and will naturally depend on your life situation, mood, and personality. If you're young and hungry, then staying up to date with the tip of technology might enable you to hop around jobs, make top dollar, and remain a hot commodity in the system. If you have a mortgage and are looking to chill, then keeping the status quo going and continuing to do a solid job at work could be your priority; you probably don't need—or want—to become an AI/self-driving car/Internet of Things/cryptocurrency master.

In my opinion, the most practical and realistic way to stay comfortably relevant is to position yourself in the right environment. There is only so far you can progress if your job description is "maintain code from 1995." The frustrated email author still had a major asset: he was a software developer for the legendary IBM. On paper, this is very impressive—many people would kill to be in his position.

Employment at a big corporation can be a luxury. There are many options for work across a diverse set of teams and projects. Compare that with a startup where the execution of a small set of goals takes precedence. If you don't like the work, you're out of luck. I am totally positive that IBM has teams in every facet of technology, from mind-numbing legacy code maintenance to quantum computing. What could the emailer do within IBM to position himself better? In the unlikely scenario that there were absolutely no other opportunities for more progressive work at IBM, then it might be time to look elsewhere.

The importance of environment is rooted in basic biology. You, me, your developer colleagues, Elon Musk, Bill Gates, we're all human. For each waking day, we all have a tank of energy points that get slowly depleted until we wipe out. Despite what anyone might say, it's not feasible to work at one-hundred-percent velocity for sixteen to eighteen hours a day. Mother nature does not work that way! One person might be more efficient than you with their tank, but at the end of the day, everyone has a limited supply of energy. By the time you get home from your regular nine-to-five job, your tank may easily be running on low. You might not have enough gas to work on those side projects.

This is why your environment is crucial. Your work situation will use up a lot of your energy. Your energy expenditure must be aligned with what you actually want to work on. Many of us will never achieve a perfect alignment between the two, but we have the power to get them into the same ballpark. The alternative scenario is very bleak—spending your energy on things you don't care about. This isn't enjoyable for anyone.

A switch in environment, even if it's not perfectly aligned with what you want, can significantly improve how you feel about your time use. This may mean switching to a neighboring team, transferring departments, or moving to a brand-new company. Take drastic measures if you have to, in order to align your energy with the right environment.

There's Too Much to Learn

In his email, the author listed over ten different technologies that he felt he needed to master. The list was a hodgepodge of languages, frameworks, and general concepts—he was paralyzing himself with so many options.

This is not ground-breaking advice: you must laser in and focus on fewer things. Humans operate concurrently. When we take on too many tasks, none of them are done well. Just like a CPU, context switching is an expensive operation for our minds.

> *Just like a CPU, context switching is an expensive operation for our minds.*

This "option overload paralysis" syndrome is pervasive in software, due entirely to the sheer number of implementation possibilities. There are a million ways to do one thing. Furthermore, we have millions of biased opinions to accompany them. Don't get distracted by all these learning permutations. Focus on less, get more done.

Biology

Setting yourself up to learn ten things means setting yourself up for disappointment. Often, we are the root cause of our own frustrations; we stress, over-complicate things, and make simple things difficult. As easily as we can become frustrated, we can lift our moods. You'll be surprised by how much is in your control—it's all about setting yourself up for the small wins.

Our emotions originate from signals and neurotransmitters in our brain. All those complicated moods and feelings are chemical reactions. For those of you who enjoy living on the wild side, you're already aware of how that chemistry can be artificially manufactured. Be careful—borrowing energy and happy moods don't come for free! For the rest of us conservatives, there are a number of natural ways to encourage those dopamine highs. I'm not talking about Instagram hearts or Facebook likes; I'm talking about shipping your app, passing the test suite on your coding assignment, and squashing a tricky bug—those are true moments of happiness for coders.

These wins can easily be replicated. A good place to start is with to-do lists. Besides their primary organizational purpose, I believe the main benefit of the to-do list is to give humans that warm, feel-good sensation that comes with checking something off. The progressive completion of a set of tasks is the foundation of how we execute. Everything from your coding assignment, to your workout agenda, to your weekend errands are just lists of to-do's. That feeling of crossing off a task that you've assigned yourself is a manufactured dopamine injection—and it feels really good.

I receive many questions about how to handle extremely large endeavors. People are unsure how to go about learning a whole new language or how to make a 180-degree career transition into software. These tasks are way too big in scope! Our brains are not wired to fathom them, let alone complete them.

This is why we always, always have to break things down into manageable chunks. Not only is this the practical thing to do in terms of execution, but it has the side effect of providing those small wins that our brains need to keep going. Next time you feel intimidated by your own goals, break them down and enable yourself to be rewarded; it's all engineering and it's all completely within our control.

Imposter Syndrome

The email author showed signs of budding imposter syndrome. Let's first give him props—he achieved his current role of IBM software developer without going through the conventional CS degree route. Software has always had its roots in academia and is often associated with higher education. This lingering historical sentiment can be at odds with the newfound accessibility of learning software; more and more people who've made professional flips into software feel like imposters compared to their four-year-CS-degree counterparts.

Let's say you got a degree in civil engineering, but made the switch and are now working as a developer. Despite the job title, you feel a mental drag because your background isn't "pure." When these feelings bubble up, remember that the civil engineering part of your life is over! If writing code is your job, I'm assuming that software has taken precedence over anything civil-related.

The only thing you have to focus on is being the best developer you can be right now; this means focusing on the present, on yourself. You already know not to compare your progression with that of others. You can dabble a little in the past to reflect on your mistakes or a little in the future to set up your goals, but the present is home base.

Sticking to the Basics or Following Trends?

Finally, the author signed off his email without any clear ideas about the future. He was torn between two options. On the one hand, he wanted to stick to the foundation, not blindly follow the trends, and keep things basic. On the other hand, he was becoming increasingly anxious about getting left behind.

By now you know that I always preach foundation. But remember that having good foundation doesn't mean you can ignore the trends—you have to do both simultane-

> *...remember that having good foundation doesn't mean you can ignore the trends—you have to do both simultaneously.*

ously. If your foundation is strong on computing and software, then you can afford to reach out and dabble in some trends. However, if your foundation is weak, you'll find yourself lost and stumbling if you reach too far.

Completely ignoring the trends is dangerous. Justifications like "that's going to die soon" are cop-outs. Remember that everything that's considered foundation today was once a trend—C++ was not always C++. Do you think you could have brushed off Java as too trendy back when it first came out? You really don't know what will stick around. Always work on your foundation and simultaneously pay attention to the trends. Change is a part of software and life. Trends come and go, but that doesn't mean you can neglect them.

34: Aligning Yourself With A Startup [Career]

This chapter is dedicated to anyone contemplating joining a startup. These ideas are based entirely on the world of small companies and are mostly irrelevant when looking at huge corporations. You join big companies for the brand, the benefits, and the free food—there's not much to think about in terms of alignment. Google has a million things going on, and a well-aligned role is waiting for you if you try hard enough.

At startups, you don't have such a luxury. Small companies will have a certain style and certain constraints. They will be at a very particular stage of their "business life" and will be looking to fulfill specific, explicit roles. Keep in mind that an explicit role is very different than an explicit technology. For example, a startup looking to get its minimal viable product off the ground is going to need a software generalist to put the disparate pieces together. This leads to a fundamental question—is an explicit role aligned with what you want? The answer will never be obvious, but it's very important.

Founder Style

Influence from the top always trickles down. The style, background, and personality of the founders significantly affects the entire company.

The style, background, and personality of the founders significantly affects the entire company.

When you're applying to startups, put in the research and find out all you can about the founders. A person with a sales background will run a company very differently to a computer scientist from MIT.

Is it Tech-Driven?

My definition of a tech company is one where the technology *is* the product. The performance of the company directly corresponds to a technical product it builds. Be extremely strict with this definition, because many businesses will falsely advertise themselves as tech companies just to keep up with the trends.

A Software-as-a-Service (SaaS) company is a tech company. Examples include Digital Ocean, CircleCI, or Atlassian. Their top-line revenues and profits are directly driven by software—technology is what they sell. Walmart, on the other hand, is not a tech company. Walmart is a retail company. However, Walmart probably employs hundreds, perhaps thousands, of software developers and pays them handsomely. You might be working as a developer in Walmart's engineering department, but you can't in good faith say you work for a tech company. Make sure you clearly delineate between companies that use tech as a complementary service and companies whose core product and service *is* tech.

I'm not saying that tech-driven companies are the best way to go; I've had some amazing experiences and gone through tremendous personal growth working for "business" companies. Do not underestimate the power of finance, marketing, sales, or any other non-technical discipline. As a developer, there are countless challenges to solve in any company, and cross-disciplinary skills can give you a serious leg up against other coding purists.

At the end of the day, you have to ask yourself—is this company driven by a technical product or not? Remember, neither is better, they are just different, but the distinction must be clear! Be aware of the true nature of the beast you're about to join.

Short-Term & Long-Term Goals

When joining a startup, pay careful attention to both its short and long-term goals. Understanding these goals isn't easy, but you owe it to yourself—and the company—to try to fully understand them. Do they want to liquidate as fast as possible? Do they really want an IPO? How technical are the products going to be? How would the engineering team look in a year? In five years? Any honest startup will answer those questions if you ask.

If a startup needs someone to build its tech from the ground up, and you've been dying to develop code from ground zero, then it might

Make sure you differentiate between healthy salesmanship and false promises.

be a match made in heaven. However, that opportunity would be a serious misalignment if you're looking to chill on the beach by five o'clock every evening. If the company really needs to develop their Android application, then there's no reason for you to be there if you want to get system-level experience. What does the company need and what do you want?

The needs of the company will be in constant flux. Small companies need developers for very different reasons than medium or large companies. Similarly, you are human, with your own set of dynamic needs. There will be a period in your life when you want to learn a specific platform, then another period when you want to do some architecture, and then another when you want to get into management. Match-making two moving targets is not a trivial task. No one's expecting them to be in perfect harmony, but they're going to have to move in the same general direction for both sides to have a chance of success.

As a reminder, be wary of excessive salesmanship when considering any employment. Startups have an uphill recruitment battle to fight, and it's highly likely that you are being sold to. There's no harm in a little salesmanship; you are a hot commodity and startups need to do whatever they can to get you on board. Make sure you differentiate between healthy salesmanship and false promises.

Have an honest conversation with any potential employer to understand their short and long-term goals. Be careful—don't take what they say at face value. Instead, listen to what you're being offered and allow yourself to form your own opinions about their goals. Then match those goals with your personal objectives until you're ready to make a decision.

Engineering Team Growth

It's imperative to get a sense of the engineering team's current state and its plan for growth in the coming years. Is this a team that is going to stay super lean, or is it about to explode? If the team remains tiny, you will take on massive responsibilities and have to fulfill every technical role under the sun. If the team is about to blow up, prepare yourself for chaos and growing pains.

Ask yourself—does the company even need the engineering team to grow? Refer back to the concept of tech company versus non-tech company. Based on that differentiation, a company's basic technical needs will be different. Those basic needs will correlate to the team requirements of an engineering department. It could

range from a few highly paid developers to a fully staffed crew. The current and future growth of engineering will have a direct impact on your experience—pay attention to this.

What Needs to be Built? Does it Fit Your Goals?

What does the startup need to build? Align the answer to this question with your technical goals. If you really hate developing web applications, then there is no reason for you to consider working at that new social network start-up. If you want to do one hundred percent JavaScript, then there is no reason for you to consider working at that new network security startup.

> *The easiest, fastest, and most time-efficient way to push out your technical goals is to align them with the genuine requirements of the startup.*

Understanding what tech the startup needs built is the most convenient—and most accurate—way to get a feel for your potential day-to-day. Throughout our entire careers, we will constantly set technical goals for ourselves. If you join Google, you'll probably be fulfilling these goals through your side-projects. However, the story is different with startups. The easiest, fastest, and most time-efficient way to push out your technical goals is to align them with the genuine requirements of the startup.

Conclusion

The decision to join a small company is significantly more personal than the decision to join a big company. The Facebooks of the world provide the highly tangible, lucrative benefits; you get a brand, you get a big paycheck, you get real stock, and you get a fancy office with dessert carts. The decision to join the tiny startup will never be so clear. If you're considering it—take, your, time.

35: Who Do We Need To Hire? [Daily Life]

Hiring is a challenging and never-ending aspect of the software industry. It's painful and tiring for the applicants; it's time-consuming and expensive for the employers. Both parties are futilely trying to find the perfect match in a system with a million changing variables. A match today inevitably turns into a parting of ways tomorrow. Companies change, people grow, requirements shift, and all we can do is appreciate the shared time while it lasts.

Companies change, people grow, requirements shift, and all we can do is appreciate the shared time while it lasts.

Whether you're a CEO looking to hire your first set of software developers, or you're a programmer looking for an environment switch, it's crucial to understand the context of a software hire. Hiring is laborious and omnipresent, but its end goal is simple and static—get everyone on the bus, get them into the right seats, and get the bus to the next stop.

The most obvious matching criteria is your technical skill. Another easy one might be the personality match or the culture match. These things are basic and I won't discuss them here. What I do want to talk about, though, is the *context* of the hire. What is the circumstance of the company? Who do they need? What do they need to get done? Does the role they're hiring for match what you want to do?

We Need an Expert in XYZ

This is the most relatable situation for any developer. You get matched with positions based on your expertise, and it's more or less a one-to-one connection. This is the startup that needs to start their iOS app, so they recruit an iOS specialist. This is the healthcare company that needs a data scientist to parse through their growing warehouse. This is the scaling finance startup that needs a dedicated security professional.

The circumstance for an expertise hire is cut and dried. The company knows what it needs, so it knows who to hire—simple. However, simple does not mean easy. You'd be surprised how often people aren't sure what their companies even need in the first place. Companies can only hire established experts after they create established roles. Smaller companies need flexible technologists; an expertise hire too early is almost always the wrong move.

We Need Someone to Execute Everything

The jack-of-all-trades generalist is a requirement for the budding startup; they need something built, as fast as possible, with as few people as possible. This is getting your MVP off the ground to start your company. This is joining up with your MBA friend to help prototype his

If you find yourself in this role, it can be exhilarating, because you will be designing everything, learning everything, and controlling everything.

or her idea. This is joining the five-person team, so you can end their reliance on Excel and WordPress.

The premise of this role is execution. The company is too young to have concrete expertise roles like Site Reliability Engineer (SRE) or Quality Assurance (QA). You can forget about management and real career feedback cycles. They need code written and they need a developer to do it.

If you find yourself in this role, it can be exhilarating, because you will be designing everything, learning everything, and controlling everything. You will get a taste of the whole gamut of software from scaling, to security, to product, to internal tools, to workflow. You'll write more lines of code than you've ever written in your life. If you've been in a silo—only working with one language or one platform—then a jack-of-all-trades role can be surprisingly eye-opening. This role is optimized for learning, impact, and sprinting. It is not optimized for longevity, compensation, or chilling.

We Need Someone for R&D

Some roles are designed for the academic and research-minded. These roles are exploratory and are built on the premise of patience, discovery, and innovation. The company chooses to spend extra capital on engineering something that has no immediate return on investment.

These roles come with few deadlines and offer the freedom to choose what you work on. If you are a technical purist, don't care for deadlines, and enjoy interacting solely with other engineers, then this role is a great fit. If you love working on product, appreciate cross-department interactions, and like to see your code get into the hands of customers, then be sure to avoid R&D.

You see these roles in both huge corporations and startups. Every company values R&D differently. Visionaries put it high on their priority list, while operational types punt it to the back burner. Big players need to keep innovating to stay ahead of the curve; thus, an R&D budget is a smart and reasonable investment. Startups—depending on founder style—either use their capital to find the next one-hit wonder, or opt to focus their cash on improving known, day-to-day tasks. Companies started by engineers will generally value R&D higher than their business-minded counterparts.

We Need to Grow and Fill Out

Every company runs on its own timeline. A new business is born every second of the day, IBM is alive and well, and then there's everything in between. There are periods on these timelines where companies prioritize growth, aiming to up the employee headcount, expand into new markets, and, most importantly, increase the value of the business.

During a growth phase, companies need resources and bandwidth to fulfill their promises. This is when you see new faces every other day around the office. Hiring is on full throttle, structure is formed, and outside consultants come in to formally train you about Agile development. During these times, growing engineering departments will open up tons of software positions from site reliability, to QA, to infrastructure, to product. If you're a specialist, this might be your time to shine. Companies know what they want and will start hiring more for expertise and less for generality.

These times are exciting for both the company and the developers. It's not the wild-wild-west anymore, and you can finally put your skills to good use. All work counts as gold during growth; you won't have to worry about Big Brother axing your project or being assigned to maintain legacy code. Even though growth periods can be exhilarating, remember that it's still only temporary. The fancy project you're building from the ground up will eventually turn into tedious upkeep for you or another developer.

We Need Someone to Manage

Hand in hand with growth comes management. These days, management roles should not be considered the only way people can climb the software career ladder; companies value technologists just as much as they value their managing counterparts—sometimes even more. The true builders always have the option to build; there is no longer an obligation or expectation to eventually become the boss.

> *...companies value technologists just as much as they value their managing counterparts— sometimes even more.*

Management is not a very sexy job. Nevertheless, it needs doing. No matter how cool or relaxed the advertised company culture is, a large group of people requires layers of accountability. If any prospective employer touts a flat structure where everyone is equal, be sure to run away as fast as possible. Google tried this and failed miserably.

A manager's job is just like any other and comes with its own set of tasks—hiring, firing, writing performance reviews, dealing with drama. Keeping in mind that management is the not the only way to advance your career, ask potential employers about each track and what it means. How much work does it take before you can make the decision to fork? What's the compensation difference between the different tracks? How is decision-making split between a principal engineer and a director? Don't be afraid to ask such questions; they show that you value your future. Any self-respecting engineering department will give you honest answers.

We Need Someone to Maintain the Code

Last, but not least, we have maintenance hires. Unfortunately, this is the least sexy-sounding hiring context, but it's also important. Never underestimate how long a codebase can exist. Developers come and go, but the code will live on. It's not uncommon to see a file header that dates back to the '90s. Inevitably, companies must deal with churn and hire new developers who can keep their systems operational.

These positions are not optimized for ambitious coders trying to change the world. These positions are optimized for people looking to chill and get home for dinner by six o'clock. These jobs are not about their novel technical opportunities. Before you accept a job like this, make sure there is some worthwhile benefit—serious financial upside, networking opportunities, brand-building. These positions are usually very easy to spot. Make sure you know what you're getting into.

36: Nothing In The Grand Scheme Of Things
[Daily Life]

Everything in your life takes up brain space. If it's not the day job, it's the side-project or it's the height of the surf this weekend. Shaolin monks and meditative types are able to keep their heads empty, but the rest of us mortals are a jumbled bag of thoughts and emotions. The activities we spend the most hours on correlate directly with our highest mental preoccupation. When such activities have the power to dominate our thoughts, it's easy for us to blow the little things out of proportion—that drama you're having at work isn't really a big deal in the grand scheme of things.

...whatever ordeal you're going through, it will just become another story in a couple of years—it isn't that big deal a deal

In college, I was in constant competition with my peers on a personal quest to become technically competent. In my various jobs, frustrations with my managers and silent struggles for rank with my colleagues preoccupied my thoughts on a daily basis. Work stress invaded my weekends. I'd complain to my parents, friends and anyone else who would lend me an ear.

If I've learned one thing from all of this, it's that whatever ordeal you're going through, it will just become another story in a couple of years—it isn't that big deal a deal. Nevertheless, what might now appear trivial was, at the time, enough to fill me with anxiety. This is something we all go through.

The stress of any situation usually traces back to the same root cause—your interaction with other humans. You will never, ever get along with everyone. There's no use in trying and, frankly, it's a completely unreasonable expectation. At the core of your mini-dramas, there is a human struggle. You will complain when someone takes credit for your code. You will be frustrated with your manager's micromanagement. You'll be upset when your founders decide to pivot the company. You'll be angry with another developer just because you feel like it. Whatever it is, it's taking up space in your brain, it's using your energy, and you're blowing it out of proportion.

Every single moment we experience is a fleeting one; you can't hold onto it. All moments will pass, the joyful and the sad, and then we die. It sounds morbid, but it's true. We are here on earth for only a short period time; we should strive to build and enjoy a simple life, and then we will be done. Nothing lasts forever.

Do not confuse my sentiment with a to-hell-with-it-all one. Life is not about being indifferent. You must stay hungry, welcome competition, and strive to progress. The caveat is that we must not become overly attached to the outcome. A friend once told me that between the ages of twenty-eight and thirty-one, he was blindly consumed with the desire to be a VP of Engineering. That position *had* to be his next step. Every job application hinged on the title, and he lost many hours of sleep over it. Blind attachment sacrifices our emotional state; it's not a healthy way of living.

There have been times when I've become so fed up with work that I've find myself complaining incessantly to friends, colleagues, and family. These thoughts took up huge quantities of my energy for weeks at a time. I would think about work on the subway, at the gym, in the shower. I was overly attached to an outcome, and had lost all focus in my regular life. It's during those moments that you have step back and remember that whatever the problem is, it is nothing in the grand scheme of things.

Do good work, don't become overly attached to the outcome, and keep your progression going.

I know that a lot of software developers out there are going through their own stressful times. I know this is easy for me to write, when I know nothing about your situation. If you are going through such times, always remember that this moment is temporary; it'll be replaced by more bad times and more good times. Do good work, don't become overly attached to the outcome, and keep your progression going.

37: Styles And Mediums [Learning]

Everyone learns in different ways. Some absorb knowledge visually, others need to get their hands dirty in the code, and a select few drown themselves in literature. Your preferred style might be the result of genetics, or it could just be how your third-grade teacher nurtured your juvenile brain.

Whatever your go-to methods are, dabbling with new techniques can provide a deeper comprehension and round out your understanding. This chapter summarizes various styles of learning—pick and choose as you like.

Learn by Doing

Just do it. This is the easiest and most straightforward way to learn anything. Start that side-project, or pick up that unfamiliar ticket from the backlog. Register for that intimidating CS class, request a transfer to a different department, or make a hard pivot into a new industry. Sooner or later, all roads of learning lead here. This is— and will always be—the bread and butter of progress. It doesn't get any simpler than this. Just do it.

Learn from a Mentor

Having a mentor is a luxury. You have found someone who has gone through what you're going through or has reached a level that you aspire to reach. A mentor is very different from a role model. A mentor gets to know the real you and provides personalized guidance. A role model is a celebrity that you follow on Twitter. A mentor will take time to understand your experiences, your level, and your outlook on the future. They'll take your context, combine it with their own journey, and use it to reflect on your life. The end result is priceless, individualized advice.

This sounds too good to be true, and it is. Many of us will never have the luxury of a true mentor. However, there is good news. We can find pieces of mentorship in a variety of places—YouTube, podcasts, books, strangers. When sifting through public resources, search for people who have shared your experiences and whose background you can relate to. The key is to have *some* level of shared experience. Without it, you become susceptible to unrealistic comparisons. If you're from China and have set your goals on coming to the U.S. to become a programmer, you're not going to relate much to the wealthy American student who takes out zero loans and gets into MIT.

In a world with billions upon billions of human experiences, you will find someone who's been in your shoes and has accomplished your goals. If you're trying to transition from developer to product manager, there are a hundred people in your city who've done it—go to a meetup and find them. If you're trying to break into coding from creative writing, there are a thousand blog posts from people who've made the switch—read them. Whatever you're going through, I guarantee that someone has gone through it, learned from it, and shared it. It's a privilege for us to have access to these resources. Dig for them.

Learn Through Research

Learning through research is the natural complement to learning by doing. Not only must you use technology, you must also study and read about it. For example, if you want to become a Node.js master, step zero will be getting your chatroom pet project off the ground. To round out the experience, spend the extra time to understand the technology's origins, its pros, its cons, and how it got where it is today. What problem was it trying to solve? What problems does it not solve? What were the major milestones for the technology? Do not put blind faith into pumping out code; it alone is not enough.

> *Not only must you use technology, you must also study and read about it.*

I categorize writing about software into two categories. There are a certain set of books that are dedicated towards the "doing." These are fifty-pound language reference books and detailed walk-throughs of frameworks. They are simple. They are concrete. They are objective. A huge book about Java is going to include everything there is to know about Java.

The second category of writing is the subjective software opinions of other developers. Many pioneers have written books with musings on computing and software as it's evolved over time. They don't care about detailing the syntax of the new C++ features, they simply want to share their thoughts about technology. In addition to writing a million lines of React code, read a blog post that hates on React, then read a blog post that puts React on a pedestal. For every software opinion you have, there's someone else who thinks exactly the opposite.

Learn from Role Models

Role models are people we look up to. We all have them, and now the Internet can give us a glimpse into their minds. Turn on your computer and you can watch Elon Musk talk smack in an interview or see candid footage of Linus Torvalds yelling at someone.

Just because Tony Robbins takes freezing baths in ice water doesn't mean you have to as well.

As I stated earlier, role models are different from mentors. While mentorship is catered to you as an individual, a role model is simply someone you respect, someone to look up to. They don't need to share your experiences or empathize with your background. Peter Theil and Steve Jobs may not be your perfect mentors, but their accomplishments still deserve our respect.

I highly recommend watching interviews, podcasts, and candid footage of your role models interacting with people. One of my favorite clips on the Internet sees Jack Ma getting the original Alibaba team hyped up about the future. He talks about the differences between U.S. tech and Chinese tech, sets an extremely high bar for his employees, and puts his foot down on Alibaba's IPO date. Just from this five-minute clip, you get a sense of Jack as a person and how he's wired. We're lucky to have that video in the public domain, and I watch it every time I need a quick injection of motivation.

Witnessing how our role models behave in the world is something we take for granted in our digitally connected age—something that wasn't so easy just ten years ago. Watching them not only serves as inspiration, but it also gives us the psychology behind how they tick. It shows us how people at higher levels operate, and it also shows us that they are still human. You will never get a sense of this from a crafted speech or a premeditated book.

Do not follow role models blindly. Just because Tony Robbins takes freezing baths in ice water doesn't mean you have to as well. Role models are a source of inspiration. They present their advice in two ways—whatever works for them, or whatever sells more books. Many people attempt to copy and paste these behaviors, and it fails them. For role models, take their knowledge merely as a resource—a rough guideline—and integrate it into your life on your own terms.

Learn Through Discussion

An amazing way to solidify your understanding of a tough topic is to discuss it openly with your peers. A solid discussion is an open forum—with open minds—participating in a mutual back and forth. This is very different from a lecture. There must be an authentic expectation for discussion.

A discussion isn't designed for you to be on the receiving end of a knowledge hose or for you to preach the gospel. It's designed to spark a dialogue over something that doesn't have a concrete answer. It's a place to uncover the pros and cons. It's a place to share light bulb moments with your friends.

Learn Through Teaching

Teaching is one of the most underrated techniques of learning. A long time ago, I was a novice C developer who somehow landed a teaching position at a summer camp teaching young high schoolers how to code. Even though I was teaching the super-noob course, I was still nervous, because I wasn't all that confident with my C.

> *Teaching is one of the most underrated techniques of learning.*

Unexpectedly, those three months turned out to be a very productive summer for both me and the kids! Teaching basic C to the students helped reinforce my own understanding of the language.

The more I explained the labs, diagrammed pointers, and debugged the students' code, the more I strengthened my own foundation.

Teaching is an art form. If you're doing it well, not only will you seamlessly transfer your knowledge, but you will also enhance your own foundation. Furthermore, teaching serves as an honest audit for your skills; if you can't explain something simply, it means you don't understand it yet. Remember, you can always learn something from someone else. Try to teach your friend about the latest JavaScript framework you picked up, then have him or her return the favor. Don't worry if you think you're not ready, you'll surprise yourself.

38: Watch The Side Effects [Coding]

Throughout your career, you will be writing a lot of code. At some point, you may fall out of love with it. And then fall right back in love with it again. I've seen developers struggle for years to get into management roles, only to willingly transfer back to being individual contributors (ICs). I've had to listen to tenured VPs tell me how the only interesting thing left in their day-to-day is squashing a bug. Coding is where it all started; it's the roots.

It goes without saying that not all code is created equal. Your code is better than your roommate's, say, but it's not on the same level as Bjarne Stroustrup's code. One thing that distinguishes the senior from the junior is their mindfulness of the side effects.

Let's talk about the aspect of coding that is new feature development. You have a stakeholder, a set of product specifications, a design template, and you're about ready to switch into dev-mode. Take

> *One thing that distinguishes the senior from the junior is their mindfulness of the side effects.*

a moment to appreciate the blessings of a new feature—most of the time, adding is significantly easier than changing, refactoring, or removing.

New feature development can lull the unsuspecting developer into a false sense of security. The grass is green, the dependencies are low, and decision-making becomes liberal. During these times, we must tread very carefully; it's dangerously easy to overlook unintended—and very serious—side effects.

A software system is in a perpetual state of change. Hundreds of developers add, delete, and modify thousands of lines of code every day. Understanding your own changes is basic table stakes. Understanding how these changes affect the system—from now and into the future—is what separates you from others. Here are some common areas where you must stay extremely vigilant—incorporating new third-party libraries, touching any interface across processes, changing any kind of serialization, changing any kind of deserialization, updating any dependency, barely modifying a query, trying to cache new data. There are too many things to list. Every single line of code requires your utmost attention.

To expand on that, ask yourself these questions. Does this change make development harder for my colleagues? Does it require a workflow change? How would this change affect everyone else's local environment? Who would want to talk about this change? Is there parallel work going on that affects this? Not all changes live in code. Don't underestimate your work's ripple effect; see it in advance.

Let's examine a concrete example. For anyone out there that's using relational databases, I'm sure that some of it is managed through an Object Relation Mapping (ORM) library. ORMs don't quite bake you the full cake, but they come pretty close. They are incredibly useful libraries that kill a lot of cumbersome boilerplate. For the majority of use-cases, ORMs work just fine and product can be shipped. However, there can be times when these libraries won't get the job done, and custom SQL must be written. If you enjoy picking away at and timing the execution of SQL blobs, then all power to you! The world needs more people like you. But in my humble opinion, ORMs beat out handwritten schema and queries any day of the week. Remember that black-boxed software magic is a double-edged sword. ORMs are rife with potential side effects—they've tripped me up many times.

External libraries encapsulate a lot of functionality away from you—as they should. An ORM can guess when you need to eager load, it'll be smart about caching associations, and it can suggest missing indices. Despite the magic, we must not ignore how they actually work. When I first went diving into web development, I was asked to make a seemingly simple change to an ActiveRecord query. I made the change with only a couple lines of code, but the cascading side effects were devastating. A couple innocent lines of Ruby code turned into five extra joins, extra seconds of execution, and a big problem for production.

I messed up in two places. First, it was obvious that I still didn't really understand our system. I wasn't aware of all the use-cases that flowed through this query's code path, and I didn't have a firm grasp of our schema. Unless you built a system from scratch, none of us can know all the nuances of a project. Every codebase has a long history filled with deprecated features and failed refactors. This history takes time and effort to understand. Put in the hours of research until you understand the subtleties of your codebase. If it's too much to fathom, ask your neighbor—he or she will have no problem telling you the war stories. A two-line change may not be as simple as you expect! All of this is to help you watch out for the side effects, which enables you to make robust updates to the system, and turns you into a higher-value developer.

Second, this mishap showed that I had not fully grasped what the ORM was doing. Why exactly were these lines triggering extra SQL? What could I have done to keep the performance the same? How was this ORM even generating its SQL? Do not put blind faith in external libraries to do everything for you in the best way possible. Third-party libraries have their own bugs, nuances, and side effects that you must understand. The moment you decide to take on a library, you own it.

> *Code is meant to be shared and loved. It's not just your code—it's everyone's code.*

This is a lesson in details. Take care of the details in your work, and be aware of the details in the side effects; very rarely does your code only affect what you want it to affect. This lesson isn't designed to scare you. You don't want your code to exist in a silo. Code is meant to be shared and loved. It's not just your code—it's everyone's code. Good software teams work collectively to elevate an entire system. Your code should have side effects, but they need to be positive side effects! As you familiarize yourself with any codebase, stay vigilant and be sure that your improvements benefit everyone. The details are what matter and what separate you from everyone else.

39: Communication [Career]

Every developer job posting requires applicants to have Excellent Communication Skills. Sounds cookie-cutter and cliché—but what exactly does it mean? Is it enunciating words clearly? Is it speaking at least once during meetings? Is it another way of saying you should always be giving killer presentations?

A good communicator is someone who can effectively explain their thoughts and keep their peers updated about everything that's going on. Seems simple, yes, but it's a skill that takes time to develop. How do you choose your words? How did you introduce the context? How do you prepare your code reviews? How quickly can you explain your work? Is your project progressing or lagging? How does your colleagues' body language change when you're around? How would you describe your tone?

People underestimate the power of communication. Not only does it serve its functional purpose of disseminating information, but it also acts as the necessary precursor to gaining respect. Pay close attention to others and develop your communication skills. It will pay huge dividends in your career.

Express Yourself Clearly on All Platforms

You must articulate your thoughts clearly on all platforms—emails, meetings, presentations, code reviews, messenger, direct speech. We discussed emails earlier, but the detailed *how* behind all these platforms is out-side the scope of this book. Place a sincere effort into each and every one of these mediums.

Everything you produce—from an instant message to a code review—must show clarity. For digital messaging, ensure your tone is respectful and your intention crystal clear. Use as few words as possible, pace the conversation, and refrain from dumping paragraphs of technical text into an unsuspecting chatroom.

For code reviews, ensure your code is nicely wrapped up with a ribbon. Don't put up a thousand lines of gar-bled red and green that barely got your feature work-ing. Don't continue developing and committing to a live review. Your pull requests should have a well-defined purpose, include documented "gotchas," and let nine-ty-nine percent of the code speak for itself.

Always Prep Before the Conversation

A huge percentage of our communication will be asyn-chronous. You have the afternoon to set up your code review, you can take three minutes to respond to an im-portant message, and you have a whole evening to write a well-thought-out email. Where asynchronous com-munication is convenient, ex-pressing yourself in real-time can be challenging and stressful. We're talking about those weekly meetings, the

> *Effective discussions start before the discussions even happen.*

design discussions, retrospectives, and day-to-day peer programming sessions. Even though you might prefer to skulk in your cave, you won't always be able to lock yourself in a cubicle pumping out code 24/7. Sooner or later, you will have to speak in real-time with your teammates.

Effectively expressing yourself in a live situation is a practiced skill. I can't help you with the actual practice, but I can leave you with the number-one tip that has helped me throughout the years—prepare for every, single interaction. Whether it's a big meeting or you're simply asking someone to come by your desk, you must be prepared.

Before the conversation happens, you should have already gathered all the context you need. It should be fresh in your mind. Effective discussions start before the discussions even happen. Once you get into that meeting room, the only unknowns left should be the ones the meeting is about to uncover. So many valuable engineering minutes are wasted due to someone's lack of context and preparation. Not only is this wasted time, but it's just a bad look. Great preparation begets seamless communication. Don't forget about it.

Body Language and Respect

Another essential part of communication lies in the receptiveness of other parties towards you and your thoughts. A lot rides on your body language and *how* the words come out of your mouth. Not many of us are psychology experts, but we should all understand and appreciate its teachings.

For example, turning your entire body towards your counterparty has a huge positive impact on an interaction.

There are certain basic rules to good conversation. For example, make sure you pause at least two to three seconds before responding. This shows that you have digested what has been said, thought about it, and are actually responding *to* the other person. If you speak too soon, or cut someone off before they've finished, it suggests that you were itching for an opportunity to get your point across. It makes it obvious that you were never actually listening in the first place. Even if you were, you've made no attempt to understand the speaker. Often, your mind will arrive at a response within five seconds of a conversation starting. Your thoughts can wait. Be respectful, be patient, and let them finish.

Another easy conversation life-hack comes through the art of the paraphrase. Paraphrasing your counterparty's words is a sign of respect, demonstrating that you are trying to understand their perspective or argument. It gives them a minute to reassess their position. It gives you a moment to solidify your own understanding, while considering a measured response.

The premise of good conversation is a mutual respect between all parties involved. For this to happen, you must—must—follow the rough guidelines of acceptable human interaction. I've seen a lot of developers with undeveloped social skills who find themselves constantly rubbing people the wrong way. They are all nice people at heart, but their lack of social awareness causes them problems in their professional life. Stay conscious of this; you will receive no formal training in the art of conversation.

Most people learn the hard way, but the simplest things make the biggest differences. For example, turning your entire body towards your counterparty has a huge positive impact on an interaction. At the same time, quickly checking your phone or dozing off during your colleague's presentation will quickly put you in someone's bad graces.

Once you are comfortable talking to others in the workplace, you may dig deeper into the art of persuasion. Remember, there is no true reality; everyone interprets the world differently. Persuasion must be built on mutual respect—you listen to the people you hold in high regard. More importantly, never attempt to be persuasive without having a foundation of respect. It never works and can easily come off as aggressive.

Don't underestimate this aspect of software development. Psychology, body language, and the tiniest of habits are all contributing factors in your ability to communicate effectively. Read a few good books, watch some YouTube, and consciously practice for a few years—you'll be all set.

Avoid Being Passive-Aggressive

Passive-aggressiveness reigns supreme among non-productive and frustrating behaviors. It benefits no one. The core reasons why people revert to passive-aggressive behavior are very personal. You will never truly understand the root cause of someone else's behavior. It could be their upbringing, a weird high school friend, or maybe a traumatic experience with a demanding boss—you can't expect to fathom it. Whatever the situation, your own behavior is always your responsibility. Passive-aggressive behavior can be extremely counterproductive; you should try to avoid it at all costs.

Passive-aggressiveness is difficult to define. If you have a friend who has worked in HR, he or she may be an invaluable resource in this arena. I've found that it is best understood through experience. Symptoms include lack of eye contact, poor body language, purposeful avoidance, and unpleasant subtleties in language. It never feels good to be on the receiving end of these.

These signs are easy to spot in others, but harder to spot in yourself. You may unwittingly be exhibiting passive-aggressive behavior. Re-analyze your past interactions with others that didn't quite feel right, and reevaluate your actions. What could you have done differently? Did you inadvertently cause tension? Were there any micro-aggressions? How might your body language have been perceived? You can't diagnose passive-aggressiveness in others if you can't diagnose it in yourself first.

Once you are armed with the knowledge and experience of this type of behavior, you must actively remove it from your personality. Passive-aggressiveness can ruin your reputation and rapport with all of your colleagues. If you don't address it soon, it will be ingrained in your behavior. The longer you leave it, the harder the habit will be to break.

Bookmark Conversations

As developers, our job requires us to have numerous concurrent conversations running throughout our day-to-days. You might be involved in a software architecture discussion, a UI back-and-forth over the latest landing page with the designer, and a road-mapping discussion with your PM. For each of these conversation threads, you will inevitably need to context-switch between them and it can be jarring.

An effective communication hack is to actively "bookmark" each individual conversation. Remember to save the context of each discussion. How did you last leave it? What was unresolved previously? What new information can you bring to light in this conversation? People actively do this for meetings, but you can do it for every single interaction.

No one likes to repeat themselves. It's a pet peeve for everyone on this planet. As a clear-headed developer, you must be on point with all of your conversations. If you forget to bookmark, it implies that the previous conversation slipped through your memory, or, even worse, you didn't even consider it important. Pay attention to conversation bookmarking and it will put you ahead of the curve.

40: Wrapping It Up

The simple act of sharing is severely underestimated; just one simple, relatable story can help someone out tremendously. I hope you found some of that here in this small sampling. To end, let's recap.

Whether you're software-for-life or just dipping your toes, put in a sincere amount of effort to hone your craft. Writing software, and writing it well, are the roots. On the technical side, revisit foundation, pay attention to details, and be open to new ideas. On the softer side, understand psychology, interact effectively with your fellow developers, and be respectful towards everyone.

> *The simple act of sharing is severely underestimated; just one simple, relatable story can help someone out tremendously.*

Never compare yourself with others. Accept that there will always be other people, on their own timelines, who are ahead of or behind you. Just focus on your own progression.

Everything in life must have balance. You are not going to become a one-hundred-percent, 24/7 software developer—actually, you won't be one hundred percent anything. Make sure you keep up your relationships, your hobbies, and your health as you pursue your goals. There is a yin and yang to every level of life. Balance your front-end skills with your back-end skills. Stay late in lab on the weekdays, then go outside and get some exercise on the weekends. Learn some accounting; take some breaks from coding. Balance is the key to longevity—nothing hinges on a singular outcome. Don't be attached to the idea of becoming the perfect developer. It won't happen and it's not healthy.

You must set goals. Many of us—myself most definitely included—can't articulate our true passions. Even though our life purpose is elusive, setting and achieving goals is tangible. The best archer in the world can't hit a target without knowing where that target is. Your goal could be to work alongside Elon Musk, or it could be just to finish that React tutorial. Keep them in focus and don't take on too many. The presence and clarity of your goals will provide your day-to-day progressions, and those all add up.

Set up clear expectations for yourself. What do you want out of software? Is it going to be your new life's work, or do you just want to gain some leverage at your current job? What do you want out of this job? Is it to accelerate your experience, grow your pedigree, or make money?

Set up clear expectations for the people around you. What do you expect from your subordinates? What about your boss? What about your friend you're about to hire? Be explicit about your expectations and communicate them early.

Expectations set up your mindset and influence your path. If you truly want to make a career out of this and get paid to write code, the journey you take will be very different from one in which coding is just your side hobby. Keep your expectations crystal clear.

Everything needs personalization. No matter what self-help books you read or what inspirational YouTube videos you watch, remember that your context is your context alone. You know your mind, your personality, your responsibilities, and your financial situation. We don't need someone else to tell us that. Find mentorship in different places, and use role models for convenient doses of motivation. You will never—ever—get a perfectly individualized solution from the outside. There is no perfect programming language, framework, or solution. Get used to internal reflection, cultivate self-awareness, and avoid absolutes.

Finally, all your work-related issues are *nothing* in the grand scheme of things. It could be a fight with your coworker, a dispute with your boss, or a flurry of passive-aggressive code review comments. Whatever it is, every obstacle you encounter will inevitably become a story in a few years. No matter how bad a situation may seem, there is always some good that you can uncover. Stay grounded and don't let these temporary fires get to you. This is the key to having a long-term healthy mindset.

Thank you for reading this book. Enjoy your journey and please feel free to reach out with any questions! My email is davex.inc@gmail.com.

Made in the USA
San Bernardino, CA
25 January 2019